THE WINNING TICKET

Dear Kim,

Thank you for being so responsible and honest in your dealings, and for being a good friend to Sonia and me.

Best of luck and have a Merry Christmas.

Stephen & Sonia

THE WINNING TICKET

What Your Grandparents Learned
about Money the Hard Way, and Why
You Need to Know It More Than They
Did

Stephen C. Johnson

VANTAGE PRESS
New York

Published by Vantage Press, Inc.
516 West 34th Street, New York, New York 10001

Manufactured in the United States of America
ISBN: 0-533-12008-X

Library of Congress Catalog Card No.: 96-90342

0 9 8 7 6 5 4 3 2 1

Contents

Prologue   vii

1. A Strong Defense   1
2. Doggie Bits   6
3. Where is There?   14
4. To Each His Own   19
5. Surf's Up!   32
6. The School of Hard Knocks   36
7. Too Much of a Good Thing   42
8. A Little Here, a Little There   45
9. Plant a Good Seed   53
10. Automania   60
11. A House Could Be a Home   71
12. Squirrels Do It   83
13. What God Hath Joined Together   102
14. A Look in the Dark Crystal   113
15. It's Not the End of the World   128
16. A Few Dollars More   138
17. Just to Be Sure   145
18. One Last Check   154
19. Try Me One More Time   160
20. Flight Plan   165
21. Of Kings and Nations   169
22. So How Would I Know?   177
23. A Few Last Thoughts   185

Epilogue   195

Prologue

I could thank so many people who have made this endeavor possible, but I thought that I should single out the one person who probably contributed more than any other: I would like to thank the babysitter we had when I was about seven years old. It all started when I strolled into the kitchen and asked, "What-cha playin'?" She replied, "Poker. Ya wanna play?" Two hands of five-card draw later I'd lost twelve cents, including the four cents I'd had to borrow from my brother. At the tender age of seven I learned, as a result, the ruthless nature of financial bondage. I'm sure that, had my parents found out, they would have been upset and set things right. For my part, I will be forever grateful they didn't!

THE WINNING TICKET

Chapter 1
A Strong Defense

Sheer terror coursed through his veins as the soft glow of the embers revealed three pairs of eyes less than thirty feet away, watching his every move. His own eyes darted back and forth between the panting beasts lurking in the evil dark. He glanced down at the pitiful little pile of twigs and bark. It was all the fuel he had remaining of what he had collected before dark. If only he had collected the wood first, and eaten later! If he had, he would have had enough fuel to last until daybreak. How long would it be until morning? It was impossible to tell. He pulled his Colt revolver from his holster and snapped it open. The backs of six shells dropped into view. As he turned the gun in the dim light of the dying fire, he could faintly see the backs of the six shells. All had a tiny imprint where the firing pin had hit the primer. Just to be sure, he pushed the shells out of the cylinder and rolled them in his hand. Each was empty.

Just then the sound of a deep growl made his eyes shoot back to the circling predators. One, two, three, FOUR! Where did the fourth one come from? He hurriedly tossed the last bits of fuel on the dying embers. Looking up again he could see more clearly as the beasts edged closer. Their silhouettes were barely visible by the light of the shimmering coals. The largest beast edged closer, becoming bolder with every pass-ing moment. By now he could see their fangs as they

1

growled. In desperation he pulled his pistol from his holster and threw it with all his might at the closest one. He missed, but much worse, he lost his balance. In falling, he put out his hands and landed headlong in what remained of his fire.

He quickly rolled out of the hot embers, with only superficial burns, but the tiny flame was extinguished. He pushed himself back against the boulders and stared wide-eyed into the dark. Without the fire he could see nothing, but he could hear the heavy breathing and the sound of paws scratching in the sand. Just then they lunged. He was eaten alive by the most vicious creatures of all. Creditors!

Imagine yourself in a position where you don't have enough money to pay the bills. Perhaps you don't have to imagine very hard. Imagine yourself having to decide whether you will pay the light bill or the heat, but not both. Imagine leaving your home forever and looking for a cheap place to stay because your house has been repossessed. Imagine yourself sixty-five years old, out on the street because your government supplement is a third what you expected.

Without trying to sound too melodramatic, I am extremely concerned about the financial future of both the United States and the world at large. I am absolutely convinced that as long as we, the United States of America, remain on the course we are presently on, extremely difficult financial times will be unavoidable. I don't know when this will befall the population as a whole or how events will play out, but unless you are very old, I think you can safely expect to see it in your lifetime. For some it has already happened. There are many people who are living in an unbelievably wealthy society, yet happiness eludes them as their financial problems surround them like drooling wolves.

Like the traveler in the wild, it doesn't have to be that

way. Some simple decisions you make, even the order in which you do things, can have a profound effect on your financial well-being. It isn't that hard, either. In fact, many people would greatly improve their financial situation by merely reading and implementing the first two chapters of this book! Of course, I believe the rest of the book is worth reading as well, but even a very minimal change would make a dramatic difference.

Whether you think the future will be unendingly brighter, or you expect the return of some of the extremely hard times experienced earlier in America's history—or anything in between—reading this book will help you prepare for the future. For some unfathomable reason, basic principles of family financial planning seem to be rarer than hen's teeth. Even people with degrees from centers of higher education have never been taught to manage their own finances wisely. This seems absolutely tragic to me. No wonder so many people are mired in a financial quagmire. The amazing thing to me is that financial security really isn't that hard to achieve. Yet so few people do.

I will warn you right now that this book is going to suggest that you change the way you spend your money. Changes require some effort. I've met several people who are hounded by financial problems but who are unwilling to change the way they spend their money. What they want are the rewards of discipline *before* they put out any effort. They remind me of the man who chided the sticks with which he intended to build a fire by saying, "Give me heat first, then I will light the match." May I suggest that the effort to light the match is well worth it.

After you have implemented a few of the simple rules described in this book, you may wonder why you used to throw so much money away. You may wonder how you ever lived like that. You will be free to have a peace of mind you never had before. I'm *not* saying you will be rich! If you want a get-rich-quick-scheme, you will have to look elsewhere. Instead, I will show you how to patch the holes in your wallet. Holes you may not presently know exist.

This book does two things. It teaches you how to manage your money; but, more importantly, it also helps to motivate. Some people know a few things they could do to improve their finances but just haven't gotten around to doing them. There are far more people in this group than I would have ever guessed before I started to counsel people about their finances. After years of frustration I finally figured out why this is true. My brother explained it like this: "It's hard to get excited about the concept of: 'live debt-free, die debt-free.' " He's right—it doesn't even have a nice ring to it. How does this sound? How old do you want to be when you retire—forty, fifty, sixty, seventy? Let's try this one. How would you like to have an extra $700 a month for ten years? Once you find out what you're missing, you may become very motivated.

My brother is a school teacher, but he would like to spend his summers writing books. Currently, he spends them working a second job, but his financial goal is to get far enough ahead so that he can be an author three months out of each year. The problem is, being an author doesn't pay dividends for several years, and he needs the money right now. When he makes his goal, I'll bet he'll make a good writer and enjoy life more, but first he has to get there. What are your financial goals? Have you ever thought about them?

Some people have few problems with their money but feel they ought to be able to do better. Maybe you never have to worry about bills but are worried about your retirement, especially in light of recent revelations in the news. If you are in this group, you are also in luck. I can show you some common-sense approaches to financial planning that will pay you real dividends in almost any scenario you might conceive, and possibly a couple you haven't yet. If you are in this group, zip through the early chapters, but not too fast, and concentrate on the later ones.

Well, I've dragged this out long enough; let's get down to saving money! Would you be interested in investing at 15 to 30 percent annual return on your principal, guaranteed? The next chapter will tell you how to do exactly that!

Chapter 2
Doggie Bits

If someone told me that I could get 15 to 30 percent annual return, guaranteed, the first thing I would do is put my hand over my wallet, keep my back to the wall, and make my way to the nearest exit. Nobody pays guaranteed 15, let alone 30 percent interest! If you are skeptical of such a claim, there is good reason. I would be skeptical too. So let me explain.

Since the 1930s, deposits in most United States banks have been insured by the federal government up to a certain amount, such as $100,000. When I say guaranteed, that's what I'm talking about. It's not perfect, but it's as good as you can get from any financial institution. Interest on such insured accounts over several decades has generally been somewhere between 3 and 4 percent. Long-term government bonds have averaged around 4.5 percent. Long-term corporate bonds have averaged about 5.2 percent. Between 1926 and 1990 common stocks averaged 10.1 percent. Take note that corporate bonds and stocks are *not* backed by the good faith of the U.S. government, nor by anybody else. Each time the rate of return on investment has increased, however, the risk associated with the investment has gone up as well. It's pretty obvious why I would be very dubious if someone told me I could earn 15 to 30 percent annual return, let alone a guarantee on that investment.

What I said at the end of the last chapter is a bit misleading. What I should have said is, I know how you can probably get the *equivalent* of a 15 to 30 percent investment. That may or may not be a significant distinction. The way to get the equivalent of a 15 to 30 percent return on your investment is to pay off your credit cards. It is true that you can't *earn* 15 to 30 percent return on your investment, but you can *lose* that much on an unpaid credit-card balance! And you have to work very hard to make that money back if you want to stay even.

The very high interest rates currently charged by many credit cards used to be prohibited by federal law. The law was changed specifically to allow *credit card* interest rates to rise. However, what you are paying, for the dubious privilege of being in debt, is actually costing you significantly more—more, even, than the obviously outrageous interest rate you are already aware of. If you are carrying a balance on your credit cards, you're being taken to the cleaners!

Ben Franklin said, "A penny saved is a penny earned." He was off by about fifty percent—but then again, he didn't have to worry about payroll deductions, did he? Things have gotten a lot more complicated in the last two hundred years. Now we even have to specify which penny we're talking about, don't we?

Last year, the first dollar I earned was tax free. If I had earned only one dollar, I would not have had to pay any taxes on that dollar, either to the federal government or to the state of California. But then I went and spoiled it all by earning several more dollars. The last dollar I earned was taxed by the federal government at the rate of 28 percent, and by the state of California an additional 8 percent. That means I got to keep 64 cents out of the last dollar I earned after income taxes. In the United States we have what is called a "progressive" tax. They call it that because, as you earn more money, the tax gets progressively more painful. The more money you earn, the higher the tax bracket. Therefore, as income goes up, a larger percentage of the last dollar earned goes toward taxes.

Let's suppose you took one dollar and put it in a fictitious bank at 15 percent interest. After one year you would have earned fifteen cents. But you don't get to keep that fifteen cents. You get to keep what is left of that fifteen cents after the tax man gets his share. If you invest a dollar to *increase* your income and you earn some interest, that interest was the last income you earned. Therefore, it gets taxed at the highest rate.

So let's say we put that one dollar in a bank and get fifteen cents interest. Then the tax man takes his share. He takes 22 percent of that fifteen cents. I don't have 15 percent return any more. What I have is 11.7 percent return on my investment, after taxes.

Every person has a different tax structure. Get out last year's tax forms and figure out the tax rate for your last dollar earned. You can figure it by looking at the tax tables. Before you get too depressed, let me tell you it gets even worse. Let's suppose you didn't make that dollar in a bank account. Let's suppose you worked overtime at work. If you earn that same dollar at a job, rather than as an investment, other payroll deductions will take an even higher portion. Of course, state and federal taxes are only part of your payroll deductions. In my case, when my salary goes up a dollar, I get to bring home about sixty cents. After I pay tithing to my church, I'm down to about fifty cents on the dollar. That is a considerable hunk of money. Fun, huh?!

Now let's consider your credit card. Let's assume it charges 13.9 percent. Let's also assume you are in the same tax bracket as I am. If you tried to find an investment that would pay you enough to compensate for the interest you owe on your credit-card loan, you would have to find one that pays 17.8 percent! Try to find *that* at a federally insured bank! And let's suppose interest rates go back up. What if your credit card goes up to 18.0 percent? That was common not long ago. You would have to find an investment which pays 23.1 percent! Perhaps you are in a higher tax bracket than I am. Thirty percent is not an impossible threshold for your losses. Ouch, that hurts!

Okay, okay, so credit cards are the financial equivalent of the Ninja death. The problem is that you *don't* have any money in the bank! Not even at 2.75 percent. You're broke! What can you do about it? Let me illustrate the situation you are in and suggest a solution.

Suppose you were in a row boat in the ocean a few miles off the coast. All of a sudden a bolt, which happened to fall off a jumbo jet flying overhead, smashes a hole in the bottom of your boat. Water springs instantly from the hole. You now have three choices: you can bail like mad; you can scream at the plane; or you can plug the hole in the bottom of the boat. Of course you don't have a boat patch handy, so what are you going to do? I'll tell you what I would do. I would tear off my shirt and stuff it into that hole as fast as I could. Yes, I know that if I do, I will probably get a sunburn. But if I don't, I'll drown!

Let me tell you what I would do if I owed a large balance on my credit cards. If I owed five thousand dollars, I would discontinue my cable television subscription, we would never have a family vacation beyond the city park, Christmas would cost our family no more than fifty dollars total, we would never eat out, we would only drive our cars when absolutely necessary, and our family would never make a long-distance phone call unless there was a death in the family. In other words, I would do anything legal and moral to get out of debt. And I would do it by reducing expenses, not by making more money. It would work, by the way, because my wife would support me emphatically. She doesn't like debt any more than I do.

Why am I so fanatical about debt? Because it destroys! I occasionally hear the phrase, "How much debt can you handle?" Why not ask, "How much pain can you handle?" What are we, masochists? I can think of a lot of things I would rather spend my money on than interest on a credit card. Can't you? Take out your credit-card receipts and ask yourself what you could have done with the interest you paid last year. It's tax-free money.

Why am I so down on credit cards and not on other forms of debt? I'm not. *Any* kind of debt will strangle you, as sure as I'm breathing. The problem with credit cards is that they are so convenient. You're in a store, any store. You see something you like. You have no cash. No problem, you have a credit card! You drop your card on the counter and, in an instant, you're another $165 in debt, in triplicate. Nobody I know finds himself driving past the doctor's office suddenly saying to the wife and kids, "Hey—*I've* got an idea. Let's ring up another $300 in doctor bills!"

So, how do you pay off your credit debts? You say you've tried before, but it never works. First you will need a budget. I'll show you how to do that in chapter four. One of the categories will be debt reduction. Later it will become the savings category. Pay the minimum amount to all of your credit cards and other debts except one, the one with the highest interest rate. Pay all you possibly can on this debt until it is paid in full. Once that one is paid, switch all that you were paying to the next-highest-interest debt. Keep this up until all your debts are paid. It takes time; it takes discipline; but it really is that simple.

In the last chapter I stated that you could get a lot out of this book, even if you only read the first two chapters. I just referred to another chapter to pay off your credit cards. It is true that a budget is the best way to control your money, but if you want to make me keep my word, do the following: Cut up all your credit cards; take any fixed amount you think you can manage every month, and put that toward paying off your credit cards. Do it just as I suggested. You *can* live without your cards. People have done it for hundreds of years. Either way, *pay them off.* Make it your first priority.

As soon as you are done paying off your credit cards, you can take that money and start saving for a new car! Just think, it will be just like a raise in pay, tax free! You can live without a ball and chain tied to your leg. Go ahead, do yourself a favor; pay them off as fast as you can. Remember, you still have the rest of your life ahead of you. How soon do you want to be free? Calculate the total interest you are currently paying and ask yourself, What am I getting for it? Why am I throwing that much money away?

If credit cards are so awful, why do I have those sinister little pieces of plastic? That's simple: they cost me nothing! All of my credit cards have no annual fee, and I always pay the entire balance due every time I get a bill. And, I might add, I rarely use my cards. I only use them on trips, or sometimes if an unexpected purchase is necessary. It is nice to be able to flip a card out if you have car trouble. The reason I don't do it more often is that it really isn't that convenient.

Sure, it's convenient for the store—they make a sale they may not otherwise have made. Once I pay with a card, a month later I get a statement. Then I have to get out my receipts and compare them to the statement. I have been billed at least twice for a purchase I did not make. Then I have to make my payment to the credit-card company with a check, which means I have one more check to balance when my bank statement comes. You want to talk convenient? Talk about cash. All you have to do is pull the money out of your pocket and pay the clerk. The problem with cash is that it really *is* too convenient. I'll explain how to control your cash in chapter 3.

All right, so you know all that, but when you go into a store, you just can't resist the urge to buy something. Try this: Cut out a coupon for doggie bits and rubber band it to your credit card. Then, every time you go into a store and feel the urge to buy and those purchasing juices start surging through your veins, when you get out your card you'll see that coupon for doggie bits. Think to yourself, "Would I be willing to eat doggie bits for a month to buy this?" If it is a new fishing pole or an Easter dress, the answer, hopefully, is a resounding *no!* If you are in the hot Mojave desert on July 10 and the car is leaking transmission fluid at the rate of a pint an hour, the kids are crying, and your wife is melting, the answer would probably be *yes.* I know mine would be; that's what I have credit cards for.

Why do I suggest a coupon for doggie bits strapped to your credit card? There are elderly people who haven't prepared sufficiently for their retirement who *will* be eating doggie bits for dinner tonight. If you don't get a hold on your finances, you may need that coupon!

Did you know that there are devices installed in most stores that interrupt the brain waves of shoppers to make them buy? It's a well known fact! They put them in the light fixtures. In the back of your mind they keep repeating "Buy, buy, BUY!" I know this because it has happened even to me, and I'm a real hard sell. You know it's true, too, because you have been caught more times than you want to admit, haven't you? Well, maybe there aren't little devices installed in the light fixtures, but it sure seems like it.

Has this ever happened to you? You're admiring your new purchase when your spouse walks in. He or she sees it. Then they ask, "Honey! You know we're broke! Why did you buy that thing?" You then explain, in the most impassioned terms used in or out of a courtroom, why you had to buy it. If you are honest, you give the same answer your nine-year-old son gives when he feeds one of your nice silver spoons to the disposal as it is running: "I dunno!" The fact is, you didn't even know you needed it this morning, but there you are, the not-so-proud owner of a thing-a-ma-bob! But hang on, there is a defense! You can defeat the brainwashing! Leave your card and checkbook *at home!*

Once you get outside in the clear air, the voice starts to fade. By the time you get home and the kids are out of the car eating their peanut butter sandwiches, the urge is gone. One woman, who took a six-week course I taught, later bragged that she had avoided three major purchases in one month using this technique. Each time it proved to be an unnecessary purchase. She knew that it had been because she didn't really miss whatever it was once she got home. Yet, in the store, each one had seemed so necessary. If it's really that necessary the need for it will be there tonight, or even tomorrow.

Maybe you're the kind of person who just can't resist. You would go home, get the card, return to the store, and buy it anyway. If that is really true, *cut up your cards—you have no choice. Destroy your cards before they destroy you.* Think about those doggie bits a bit more. It doesn't have to be that way. Many people plan for the future and never want for the necessities of life. Keep reading. You could be one of those lucky ones. It beats eating doggie bits.

Chapter 3
Where is There?

"This is your captain speaking. I have some good news and some bad news. Let me tell you the good news first.

"Since leaving the airport, due to a stronger than expected tail wind, we have been making excellent time. As a result, we are twenty minutes ahead of schedule.

"Now for the bad news. I regret to inform you that we are lost."

Are you lost? Do you know where you are going? Do you know what your goals are?

Have you ever noticed how hard it is to get some teenagers to do their homework, but if you ask them to clean the yard for $20, they're out there in a flash? You might well ask yourself, "Don't they get it? In the long run, doing their homework is much more valuable than $20! I wish they would catch on to how important it is to study now, while they have the chance."

Maybe the reason some young people will clean up the yard for $20 but resist doing their homework is that, while they can see the short-term rewards, they can't see the long-term financial benefits. Put yourself in their shoes. Remember when you were thirteen years old? You had been working in school for more than half your life and hadn't yet made a dime for all your effort. Well, maybe a few bucks when grades came home; but, averaged over a semester, you were making perhaps a couple of pennies per hour! Who could get excited about that? What's more, you were not going to graduate from high school for five more years, and from college for at least nine years! You were on a treadmill that never ended. Day after day you trudged to school, survived hours of boring lectures, then trudged home to slave through endless homework. Tote that barge, lift that bale.

Suddenly, you had the chance of a lifetime! You could strike it rich! In just two short hours of raking leaves and mowing the lawn, you could make almost as much as you would in a whole semester of English, math, and science! We're talking easy money, too. Hour for hour, a 10,000 percent increase in pay. Forget school—you had a get-rich-quick scheme if there ever was one. If you quit school and got a job raking leaves, you could make more money than you could ever spend!

As an adult, this seems ridiculous, because we know that youth is all too short and it must be used to prepare for adulthood. We know that a good education can literally increase our income by tens of thousands of dollars per year. We also know that the expenses of the adult world are far greater than a teenager might typically understand. But to a teenager, the world looks altogether different. Take a moment and transport yourself forward to a different time. Maybe your decisions are just as shortsighted as the teenager's resistance is to doing homework.

How much time have you spent thinking about life after retirement? Spend a day with someone who is sixty-eight years old. Do they look like they would like to go to work today? Before I was married I spent the better part of a summer with an elderly couple, and although they had the basics covered, their vulnerability due to health was obvious.

They were pretty much set, because they had prepared for old age, but it could have been a much bleaker story if they had failed to prepare.

Spend a few hours visiting with someone who has a better, more enjoyable job that requires more training. Maybe you are settling for a dead-end job because you haven't put in the effort to get a higher level of training. Are you satisfied with where you are going financially? Sit in a nice comfortable chair for just a minute and imagine what it would feel like to have all your bills paid, a car that better suits the family's needs, and, ten years ahead of schedule, no more house payments. Let these thoughts sprout roots and grow.

Does your vision extend beyond the end of your shoes? Often we get so bogged down with the here and now that we seem to forget that there is a tomorrow. Trust me—there are many tomorrows, not just one. Extend your gaze and ponder the possibilities.

When I was a teenager some nationally known commentators pontificated on the apathy of much of the nation's youth. When asked why they didn't have a more aggressive attitude toward life, these youths responded, "Oh, what difference does it make? Before I grow up the world will blow itself to bits with atomic bombs."

Well, those who survived are now in their forties. Among those who didn't survive, none died in a nuclear exchange. Most of those who, cynically, chose to drop out woke up one day and joined the human race. The strange thing is, many of them still act like it will all end in a blinding flash of light any day now. They still aren't planning for the future yet. You can't postpone planning for retirement until age fifty-five and expect satisfactory results.

Think of a football game without goals at the end of the field, no yard lines, and no out-of-bounds. How about a baseball game without bases. Try golf some time without a cup to hit the ball into. You must have goals or you can't win in the game of life. In football, you may have the ball, and the entire opposing team may be behind you as you run, but you can't make a touchdown if there aren't any goal posts to run through!

Get out a piece of paper and write down at least three financial goals you want to reach. A wise man said that a goal that isn't written down is only a wish. Never mind what the fairy princess told Pinocchio, wishes don't usually come true. But reasonable goals can be achieved. Going to school is no big deal, if you keep in mind the end result of a much better job if you stay with it. Also, the realization of how tough it is going to be if you don't get a good education can be a convincing motivator.

Maybe you are already a good goal-setter, but you just haven't applied the talent to financial planning. When you go shopping, do you make a list of what you are going to buy before you go, or do you just walk in the store and buy what you see? Setting goals is not hard, but it is a talent that takes getting used to. Generally, like everything else, the more you set goals and carry them through to completion, the better you get at goal-setting.

You're not going to change your life unless there is something to be gained in return. Before you read any further, stop and think about what goal you wish to achieve. Dwell on it for awhile. Fantasize that you have already achieved that goal. Consider what it will be like if you don't achieve the goal. Consider the two possibilities and choose your destiny. As you read this book, you will probably reevaluate and change your goals. That's fine. It should be an evolutionary process. Some of your goals will be short term, like paying off the car. Some will be long term, like investing for retirement. Work on your goals. Craft them until they feel comfortable to you. Life without goals is like a car without a steering wheel. It will be no time before you find yourself stuck in a ditch, or worse!

As you work on your finances, you will start to accomplish some of the goals you have set. Each time you do, it will give you more enthusiasm to keep working on the longer-term goals. Retirement may be twenty-five years away, and just as remote as graduation is to a thirteen-year old. Paying off your credit cards may only take fifteen months, and it is much easier to see a reward for your efforts. Be sure you make both kinds of goals, because both are important.

Too many of us make goals like buying a new car, or a new bedroom set, but don't concern ourselves with paying for them. Trust me—paying off your credit cards can bring a good feeling, just like shedding ten pounds can. Eating half a German chocolate cake in one sitting can be fun, and I've done similar things. But the price you pay is too great. Once you get in better physical shape you will feel better, you will get sick less often, and you will be able to do things you couldn't do before. In the grand scheme of things, immediate gratification is *not* the way to find happiness, and goals will help you get to where you really want to be.

"This is your captain speaking. We will be descending into the airport now. Please remain seated with your seat belts buckled and your seats in their upright position until the plane has come to a complete stop. For those of you who will continue on with connections to other destinations, you will find a map of the terminal in the seat pocket in front of you. Those who have arrived at your final destination, we wish you a pleasant stay. We thank you for flying with us, and hope your flight was a pleasant one."

Chapter 4
To Each His Own

What is a budget? A budget is a guide for spending your money. It's like a map. Suppose you wanted to go somewhere that you had never been before. Most people would get a map, find the destination on the map, and draw a line on the road they intend to follow. Then they would consider themselves ready to go. Now consider going on a trip using the same technique most people use to manage their money:

"Okay, which way do we turn now?" the father says as he comes to another corner.

"Let's go left," someone pipes up from the back seat.

"No, let's go right!" another says in a louder voice.

"If we go right, the sun will be in my eyes!"

"If we go left, I won't be able to see the mountains!"

"Right!"

"Left!"

"All right! I've heard enough." The father shouts. "We're turning left!"

"Darling!" the mother says, more than a little strain in her voice. "Why are you turning left?"

"Because I think that is the right way to go, of course!" he answers with obvious exasperation.

"Last time you turned right!"

"So?"

"If you turned right last time, why are you turning left now?"

"That was then, and this is now! Now, are you going to support me as the head of this family or not?"

"I will if you're right, but I won't if you're left."

"That does it! This trip is over! Look for a bus station. I'm going home! The rest of you can go on without me!"

Compare that to the following.

"Darling, we're coming to another intersection. Which way do we go?"

"Turn right and soon after that, turn left. You can't see it through the trees, but right after you turn there will be another turn, so merge to the left as soon as it is safe."

"Okay. Say, I'm getting a little tired. Is there a place we can conveniently change drivers?"

"Well, on the map I see a town about five minutes up the road. We could stop to eat and go to the bathroom. How does that sound?"

"That sounds fine."

Which sounds like the way you want to run your finances? I can't tell you exactly what your budget should be like, any more than I can tell you where you should go on vacation this summer. What I *can* tell you is how to read and use a financial map.

So how does a person budget? First, find out where your money is going. "We just don't understand where all the money went," is one of the most frequent comments I hear from people who seek help on their finances. Write down everything you bought and how much it cost for one month. This is not a budget; this is a damage assessment. It provides very little constraint on your spending; it only tells you where you went wrong.

Get out your utility bills, checkbook, credit-card receipts, etc., and look them over. Group them into different kinds of expenses. For example, group all of your utilities into one group and car expenses into another. A lot of information will have to come from your damage assessment, because you probably don't keep receipts for most of what you buy. Do you know how much you spent on kids clothes or snacks last year? You will if you keep track.

Once you know where your money is going, then you can figure out where you need to make changes in order to meet your goals. Don't skip over this very important step. You can't budget unless you know roughly how much to put into each category.

Now you can start your budget. Take a piece of lined binder paper and draw a line down the middle of it, top to bottom. On the left, list the categories; on the right, list the monthly dollar amount you want to go into each category. Put the categories that are most important to you at the top, and the less important ones at the bottom. The dollar amount for each category should be based on your damage assessment.

Obviously the dollar amount of your categories should add up to your monthly salary. Guess what? The first time through, it won't! You may be tempted to say, "Oh well, I guess a budget won't work for me." Wrong! This is where the work begins. A budget *will* work for you, but it won't just happen by itself.

In a rose garden there are plants that are *not* supposed to be there. They're called weeds. They may be just fine in a cow pasture, but they're not supposed to be in your rose garden. So what do we do about them? We pull them out. Guess what? That takes work, sometimes hard work. But if you want a rose garden, you can't just let anything grow that happens to come up. And, if you want to meet your financial goals, you have to weed out the expenses that are nice, but are not what you really want.

21

Don't be discouraged if this takes a while. It may seem impossible at first, but as you work at it, you will find more and more ways to make your budget work for you. There are many examples of how sustained determination can pay off, but I think my daughter Mindy is a classic example of someone not giving up when she wants something. Let me tell you, when Mindy wants something really badly, she is *one determined little soul.*

One evening Mindy insisted I take the training wheels off her bike. The next morning she got on her bike determined to learn how to ride. She knew she could ride, because she'd seen other people doing it, and she wasn't going to quit until she could ride like they did. When I came home from work that evening she was making lazy circles in the street, blowing bubble-gum bubbles as she rode. There were no signs of the struggle she had just endured, no tears, no frustration, just sheer satisfaction in the knowledge that she had overcome an important obstacle.

Mindy learned to ride in one day, because that was all she did until she was good at it. She *wanted* to learn, and was *determined* not to quit until she had mastered the skill. Budgeting may feel like a real struggle at first, but with desire and determination, you will conquer. Once you know how, it's easy.

We'll talk more about specific things that can be cut later, but for now, it is only important to make up your mind that you *will* make cuts. Remember, what you are doing is giving up something you want now, for something you want *more* later. Don't forget the importance of savings! Once you pay off your debts, if you're not saving, you're just treading water. Even if it is only $5 per month, save something! We'll talk more about savings later also.

The following is an example of a budget based on a yearly salary of $30,000 per year, of which only $24,000 per year is left after payroll deductions. This comes out to a nice round figure of $2,000 per month.

CATEGORIES	DOLLAR AMOUNT
RELIGIOUS DONATIONS	$250
SAVINGS	$100
HOUSE	$600
FOOD	$400
MEDICAL	$100
UTILITIES	$150
CAR	$200
FATHER	$50
MOTHER	$150
TOTAL	$2,000

Where is the category for movies or entertainment? Which category do diapers come from? I didn't see Christmas presents anywhere! Talk to your spouse about each category and come to an agreement about what each category includes. When my wife and I go out on a date, I usually treat. In our family, diapers, Band-Aids, and body soap come out of food. The reason we do that is because we buy these things in the same store we buy groceries. A Boy Scout book for Dad comes out of Father. New drapes comes out of House. School supplies comes out of Mother. Clothes comes out of either Father or Mother, depending on who bought them. Do it any way that makes sense to the two of you.

Wait a second! Why is it that the Mother category gets three times as much as Father? Whatever happened to equal treatment under the law? Well, it's like this—you do it your way, but in *my* family, this isn't sexist, it's reality! I don't buy the school supplies, and I don't pay for the swimming lessons. I don't pay for most of the Christmas presents, either. The point is, the two of you need to work it out and do it in an atmosphere of love and sharing. Remember love and sharing? It's the reason you got married.

Resist the temptation to make a category for everything. That makes it too complicated. The simpler it is, the more likely it is to succeed. If you have more than about a dozen categories, it is probably too complicated. Keeping track of a few categories is easier than keeping track of lots of categories, and is therefore more likely to be done conscientiously. Keep it simple.

The Car category includes gas, oil, repairs, maintenance, and car insurance. Over time, the total amount of money accumulated in the Car category should increase. Eventually you will buy a car with that accumulation. If there isn't enough going into the Car category, your present car will have to last forever, or your next car will have to be *very* inexpensive. The House category would include not only the monthly loan payment, but also a little extra for home repairs. In our family, Medical covers not only the obvious doctor and dental bills, but also visits to the vet. I didn't like that idea, but I couldn't come up with a better one. You have to be flexible.

Suppose you find some dandy little thing that your family absolutely needs. You talk to your husband or wife, and he or she doesn't agree. Your spouse thinks it's a dumb idea. No problem—pay for it out of your category. Unfortunately, if you already spent all your allotment, then you will have to wait until next month. This is how your budget keeps you from spending your savings, which someday you will absolutely need for essential, life-sustaining expenses, on the pleasures of the moment.

Now that you have your categories, get a cheap spiral or loose-leaf binder with blank pages in it. Every couple of pages, put the title of each category at the top of the page and the dollar amount next to it. We use paper clips to make it easy to flip to the category we want. Divvy up the money you currently have in your wallet, the checkbook, the top dresser drawer, or wherever it is, into the different categories and start writing purchases down.

Every time you spend money, bring the receipt home and subtract the value of the receipt from the balance of the appropriate category. At the beginning of the month, add to each category the amount allocated to that category for the month. If there is any money left over in a category, carry the surplus into the next month. If you spent less than the allotted amount for a specific category, then you will have that much more in it to spend for the next month. If you overspent in a category, you will have that much less for the next month. An example of three categories is shown on the next page:

In your budget each category would be on a different page, but here they are shown next to each other. Each column shows a running total of how much is in each category. For the Food category we don't bother to write down the type of items purchased, because it is not important to us to know the specifics. In the other two categories, Car and Father, after each dollar amount a word or two is listed so we know exactly what was purchased. This will be very important to you as you modify your budget. If someone claims there isn't enough in their category to cover reasonable expenses, they now have the documentation to support what they say. Without it, whoever shouts loudest tends to be the one who wins.

Notice that Father went a little negative at the end of May. That means he has that much less to spend in June. It's not a real big deal if you occasionally overspend a little in one or two categories, as long as you have other categories that have some money saved in them and you replenish them

FOOD $400	CAR $200	FATHER $50
146.97	783.56	4.65
-54.24	-12.50 gas	-5.95 book
-------	-------	-------
92.73	771.06	-1.30
-12.47	-146.83 brakes	+50.00 JUNE
-------	-------	-------
80.26	624.23	48.70
+400.00 JUNE	-9.75 gas	-3.62 flashlight
-------	-------	-------
480.26	614.48	45.08
-89.67	+200.00 JUNE	-12.14 film
-------	-------	-------
390.59	814.48	32.94
-43.62	-11.00 gas	-2.87 batteries
-------	-------	-------
346.97	803.48	30.07

the next month. If they *all* go negative, expect a call from the bank about that checking account you used to have.

As time goes by, two things should happen. Every category should build up at least a little reserve, and you should tailor the categories so that they are balanced. In the example above, Car is carrying a significant balance forward, but it will have to grow a lot more before a "new" used car can be bought to replace the current one.

As soon as you start to budget you will notice there are a lot of things you spend money on that you didn't notice before. Just talk about it and come to some kind of agreement about where each type of purchase should come from. It doesn't matter how you cut the pie, as long as the two of you agree and the numbers add up. As long as it works for you, it's good enough.

There are, however, two rules that need to be followed or the budget won't work. First, if you spend money, you *must* write it down! No exceptions. It doesn't matter if you spend cash, check, or credit card. Every time you buy something, bring the receipt home and subtract it from one of your categories. I like to put the receipts in my wallet as soon as I buy something so they don't get lost. After I subtract the amount from the appropriate category in my budget, I throw the receipt away, or, in the case of my credit card, file it. If I buy items in one store that go to two categories, I round off one of the values to the nearest dollar and let the other be the balance. Just be sure that the total amount subtracted equals the total amount spent.

When I buy something with a credit card, I circle the purchase in the budget book. When the bill comes in the mail, I put a check next to the circle so that I know I have paid the bill. My wife prefers to subtract the credit card bills when she pays the bill. Either way, you have one more thing you have to remember. This is one reason I prefer to use cash instead of credit cards when possible. The transaction is real simple. All I have to remember is to take the receipt home and write it in the budget book. There are no "gotchas" a month later.

You may think, *Well, I don't really want to bother writing all this stuff down, but I'll read on to see what other ideas he may have.* Don't bother. This is the essence of budgeting. Without writing down your purchases, my plan, like a plane without wings, will not get off the ground. You *must* do it! You simply have to commit to writing it down. It's like feeding the pets you may have. If you don't feed them every day, they will die. If you don't write down everything you spend in your budget book, my plan can't work.

The second rule is even more important than the first.

Before a given category goes negative, stop spending! If you want some new clothes, or a good book, you will just have to wait. The fact that there is money in your wallet should make no difference if the category is empty. If you don't slow down the rate at which you spend, nothing will change. You'll just have a lot of red ink all over your budget.

If you do it right, you really won't feel that much of a change. Usually, you will just put off for a short time a few purchases that you really want, and you won't buy some other things you really didn't need anyway. One person put it this way: Once he started his budget, he quit looking at the ads every week. He was combing the ads looking for deals, instead of buying what he needed because he needed it. Now, when he buys something, he starts looking in the ads for a deal when he really knows what he needs. He was filling his garage with a lot of neat things he really didn't need. The true beauty of a budget lies in the fact that you won't spend the house payment on a new bedroom set, or buy a fancy new car with the money you will later need for the kid's college.

When I was little, our family had a problem with bananas. Bananas were a small luxury in our family and everybody loved them. My mother would come home from the supermarket and have eight bananas along with the rest of the groceries. The time would be 1:18 P.M. It would be sunny and bright outside, and life looked good. At 4:06 P.M., when Mother went to make a fruit salad, there would be only one banana left, and all six kids would claim they'd had no more than one banana. Some would claim they'd not even had one. The math didn't add up. When Dad came home he heard about it, and inevitably, we heard about it! It was no longer bright outside and life was certainly not good anymore, either.

My father came up with an ingenious plan to deal with this problem. The next time my mother bought bananas she would write a name on each banana with a felt-tip pen. Dave, Karen, Bob, Steve, Betsy, Eric, Mother, Mother. Bananas with Mother written on them were designated for dinner, and so forth. Suddenly, as if by magic, the problem was solved. Although several of us would willingly indulge in temporary memory loss, none of us was actually willing to commit theft! What had been a furious feeding frenzy, where the law of the jungle ruled, now became civilized; and the concept of private property triumphed.

The analogy to a budget should be obvious. One category can't steal from another category if you keep track of each pot of money separately. I might add that, at first, my mother was not too wild about writing the names of her children on the side of each banana. It just seemed too untrusting. Yet anyone who runs a business knows the value of labeling and segregating. It's not just a matter of trust, but one of organization.

Every once in a while you ought to find out how much you are worth. If you're going to retire before you stop breathing, this value should be getting larger every year. The only way to know how much you're worth is to do an audit. An audit is nothing more than a total of what you own, minus what you owe.

First, add up your bank accounts, checking accounts, money in the jar on the dresser, whatever. This should equal what you have in your budget if you add the totals of all the categories. (That is another important thing to know. If I'm within twenty dollars, I call that close enough.) Add that total to the present value of your house, the value of your car if you sold it (not how much you paid for it), what you have in life insurance, and money investments like mutual funds. In other words, all your valuables. This total is what we refer to as your assets. Don't include the value of the dirty laundry or the kid's toys. If you have a garage sale nobody is going to pay much for them, even if you run them through the wash.

Next, add up your liabilities. This would include the home loan, the loan on the car, student loans, credit-card debt, doctor bills, anything you owe money on. (If you have any teenagers you could claim they are your biggest liability, but don't include them for the time being.) It is impossible to calculate how much they may cost to raise, and besides, they just may turn into an asset some day. Hope springs eternal.

Lastly, take your liabilities and subtract them from your assets. This should be a rough number. I round off to the nearest thousand dollars. Even that is probably kind of a joke, because I am estimating the price of my house to the nearest ten thousand dollars. Keep track of your total financial value. It will help you to know where you are financially. It's also the framework of what you are going to live on when you get old.

I know several people who have a messy desk or garage who claim they know where everything is. I don't believe it. Sure they know where most of the commonly used things are, enough to baffle the casual observer. Ask them to find something they haven't used for a while. Fifteen minutes later they finally find it, but five or six times during the safari of looking for it I hear them mutter, from behind a pile of boxes or as they peer into a crowded top shelf, "Well, what do you know? I haven't seen this thing in years! I didn't even know I had it anymore." Then, when they finally find what they'd originally set out for, they gleefully exclaim, "See, I knew it was here all along!"

One way of thinking of a budget is as a way of organizing your financial life. I have a drawer for socks and a drawer for underwear. In my closet I hang my pants on the left and my shirts on the right. My suit goes down at the end. You would never think of throwing all your clothes in one big box in the corner of your room and then rummaging through looking for what you need. Why treat your finances that way?

Try this experiment to illustrate my point. Add up these numbers in your head. Eight, sixty-two, one hundred and ninety-nine, fifteen, twenty-one, seventy-two, sixteen, one hundred and twenty-eight. Now try it this way. Add up the numbers below on a piece of paper.

```
      8
     62
    199
     15
     21
     72
     16
   +128
   -------
```

Which way is easier to get 521? You may think you can keep track of your finances in your head, but writing it down is actually a lot easier. That is, of course, unless you don't care what answer you get.

You may be like Christopher Columbus. He set out with a plan to discover a new way to get to the Far East and wound up in the New World. But where would he have been if he hadn't had charts and maps? He might not have even found Spain! Your budget will change over time; it has to. Your income and family needs will change. When your kids grow up, their clothes sizes change, but that doesn't mean you throw up your hands in frustration and exclaim it can't be done. Keep working on your budget. Tailor it until it fits. It beats walking around without pants!

Chapter 5
Surf's Up!

"Uh, Teach, I mean, uh, Mister Johnson?"

"Yes, may I help you?"

"Uh, like, this is all real cool, but have you got a budget that would work for me?"

"Sure. Start by recording your expenses for a few weeks to base your—"

"No, you don't get it, Mr. Johnson, your budget won't work for me."

"Why not?"

"Well, it's, like, real complicated, man."

"No, it's really not all that bad when you get used to it. See, if you keep it down to ten or twelve categories it really isn't all—"

"Like, whoa, man! That's easy for you to say, but, like, all that math stuff is, like, real hard for me to, like, figure out. Like, you catch my drift?"

"Complicated?! What's complicated about adding and subtracting?"

"Whoa! Adding, subtracting, like, how do you keep it all straight? All those numbers just start coming at me all at once, and I just can't keep them all straight! Like, you know what I mean, Teach?"

"Yes, I'm beginning to realize the scope of the problem. And you want a budget you can handle. Is that right?"

"Yeah, man, like, you're catching on. So, like, what do you think? Do you have a budget for me? One that won't interfere with my life-style?"

"How did you do that?"

"Do what?"

"String two large syllables into a single word like that?"

"Huhh?"

"Never mind. Life-style? Describe your life-style. Tell me how you currently keep track of your expenses."

"Well, it's like this. If I want something, I buy it, unless I don't have any money. Then I bum some dough off my friends. Then we all go down to the beach and check out the babes. When we get tired we, like, crash or something. It's, like, real cool, dude."

[Long pause] "Hmmm . . . you say you want a budget. Why do you think you need a budget?"

"To go to college. Like, to go to college, it takes a lot of money."

[Longer pause] "College?"

"Yeah, like my Old Man says that I got to start savin' for college or somethin' or he'll throw me out of the house, so I got to start savin' for college. My old man's over there by the punch bowl, trying to act like he isn't watching me. He made me come to this instead of hangin' out with my buds. Major bummer! Anyway, he says I have to go to college. I think I'll go to Princeton or Harvard or somethin', 'cause I want to be a brain surgeon or astrologer or somethin' like that. Besides that, my surfboard is, like, all trashed, and I need a new one, so I got to save for that too. You got a budget that will work for me?"

[Very long pause] "Yes, as a matter of fact, I think I do."

"No way!"

"Way!"

"No way!"

"Way!"

"You're jokin' me, aren't you?"

"No, but I think my brain is starting to melt."

"You have a budget that will work for me?!"

"Well, if it will work for you, it will work for *anyone!*"

"So, like, lay it on me!"

"Do you have any income?"

"Huhh?"

"Do you have a job?"

"Oh, yeah! Three hours a day I work at the pool as a lifeguard. Most of the time I just check out the babes, but every once in a while some kid acts like a submarine so's I got to, like, rescue him and all. It's, like, real cool! All the babes dig that hero stuff. Also, sometimes my Dad makes me work around the house for a while, until he gets real mad at me for no reason and gives me twenty bucks and tells me to get lost."

"Okay. I think I got the picture. I've got, like, just the budget for you!"

"Really! Cool!"

"You bet. First, tell your Dad to take that twenty bucks and put it in a bank account for you. Have him start an account in which the only way to withdraw the money is if both of you have to sign for it. That's your college fund. Also when you get paid at the pool, have them deposit twenty dollars into that same account for your college. Take them a . . . On second thought, have your Dad take them a deposit slip and they can fix it all up for you. Open a second account with just your name on it. Every time you get paid, take twenty more bucks and deposit it in the second account, the surfboard account. When there is enough in it to buy a surfboard, buy one. As for the rest of the money you make, spend it. When it's gone, stop!"

"Whoa, man! It's, like, that easy?"

"It's, like, that easy!"

"Whoa! That's cool, dude! Say! I, like, really appreciate it. When I get to be a brain surgeon, if you ever need any surgery, you come to me. I won't charge you nothing!"

"Ah, maybe you should lean more towards astrology."

Chapter 6
The School of Hard Knocks

"Excuse me, uh, I, well gosh, I guess I need some help!"

"Sure, what can I do to help you?"

"Well, I couldn't help but overhear what you told that boy. Excuse me, but were his pants on backwards?"

"I believe they were. How can I help you?"

"Well, me and the Mrs., well, you could say we're in a bit of a jam. The fact of the matter is, to tell it straight, we're plum near always in a jam. Hoo wee, I wish I had a rich daddy like that young kid you were talking to. See I hardly knew my daddy. He drunk himself to death before I was five.

"We were living down Austin way, and my mama was left with four children and hardly no way to feed them. Well, when my daddy died we packed up and left for California. We were going to the promised land, I guess, but I think mostly she just wanted to get away from the shame, everyone knowing everybody and all. My mama went from place to place trying to make the best of it, and we finally wound up in Barstow. My mama tried to teach me right, but I never made it past the ninth grade. I guess I raised a little too much . . . well, you know how boys can be. Sometimes they can get pretty big for their britches. My mama tried, but we thought we were pretty smart. Hard to teach someone when they think they know it all.

"Well, I got sent to reform school a time or two, but when

I turned seventeen I wound up in front of the judge one time too many. He gave me a choice of six months in jail or a hitch in the service. I chose the U.S. Marines, and before I knew it, I was carrying an M-14 and headed for 'Nam. Ya know, I sure hated that drill sergeant of mine, but he made a man out of me. I was nothing but a worthless piece before he got hold of me, but he taught me discipline. In the corps, you learned a thing or two, and one is, you never let your buddies down. Well, I did my tour, and when I got out I decided I was going to amount to something.

"I started driving trucks, because they'd taught that to me as a Marine. I met Shirley, that's my little lady; I met Shirley in a little town outside Tulsa in a truck stop. She was waiting tables, and I thought she was the prettiest little thing I had ever seen. Well, I courted her, and before I knew it, we were married and had a little one on the way.

"Well, that was seventeen years ago, and I haven't got five dollars more now than I had then. It seems like I make good money, but somehow I haven't got anything to show for it. I own my own rig and all, but every time it looks like I'm about to get ahead, another expense comes along and cleans us out!

"I think the main problem is, I don't make regular money like other people do. Sometimes I got all the work I can handle, but then the next thing I know the work is slim for a couple of weeks, sometimes a month or longer. And sometimes, when the money comes, we try to make up for lost time and get a little carried away. You know what I mean?"

"Yes, I think I do."

"Ya think you can help me and my little ones? You see, I have seen what it's like scratching for a living, and I want my children to have it better. They're good kids, every one. There isn't a one as ornery and good for nothing as I was.

They're good in school, too. The problem is, if I can't come up with some money, they aren't ever going to make it past high school. So, what do you say? What should I do?"

"So—the problem is your income is irregular. And when you do get some money, it seems like it just goes; and sometimes you get a little carried away trying to catch up for lost time. Is that about right?"

"Yep, you got it!"

"Let me ask you a couple of personal questions. You don't have to answer them if you don't want to. How serious are you about this?"

"Mister, this is the reason I'm here tonight to hear you speak. Just yesterday, I got home from a long haul. When I came up to the house, there was my little Valerie. She's my oldest. Well, she was just getting out the passenger side of Deke's old Ford. Now, Deke's okay, just his peak in life will be if he gets to be the manager of the Gas 'n' Go, and that's if he's lucky an' applies himself. Valerie's my little baby, and she . . . I just want to make sure she doesn't wind up waiting tables and . . . She could be so much better if I just . . ." He never finished his thought through the tears in his eyes, but he didn't need to.

"This is going to be hard. Are you willing to go through with it?"

He didn't speak, but he nodded his head and pushed away the tears with his big fists.

"Have you got any hobbies?"

"Yes, sir," he managed.

"What are they?"

"Shootin' n' fishin'."

"Would you give them up if I asked you to, to get her to college?"

"Yes sir, I would."

"Let me ask you one more thing. Have you got any bad habits that cost you a bit too much?"

He didn't answer at first, but just stared at the floor. Seconds dragged by as tears splashed on his dusty old cowboy boots. Finally, that big hunk of a man lifted his head and spoke not much more than a whisper in a quivering voice, "I guess my old man left me more than a last name after all."

"Do you drink much?"

"Not when I'm on the road. I'm no drunk. But when I'm home with nothing to do, well, every once in a while I drink a lot more than I should."

"Just when you can afford it least?"

"I guess so."

"I'm going to tell you how you are going to send your daughter to school. Are you interested?"

"I sure am!"

"First, I want you to give up the bottle. Do you think you can do it? Can you do it for Valerie?"

"Oh, sure. Sometimes I go for a month without drinking when the hauling is good. I just have to set my mind to it."

"Is it set?"

"It's set."

"Okay, I'll tell you how you're going to do it. Get a real nice picture of your daughter—a portrait, nice, but cheap—and put it in a frame. In the corner of the frame, put a small picture of the college she would like to go to. Get a patch that says *Semper Fi* and put it underneath her face. You remember what *Semper Fi* means, of course?"

"No Marine *ever* forgets *Semper Fi*. 'Always Faithful'!"

"Can you always be faithful to your goal of sending your daughter to college?"

"Yes, sir!"

"Okay, now I want you to make yourself categories just like I talked about tonight. Make them the bare bones. You're going to be making a lot of homemade beans and cooked potatoes, and no delivered pizza. Got it?"

"You got it!"

"Make one of your categories truck maintenance. Add to it just enough to pay for maintenance, oil, filters, stuff like that. No shiny hubcaps, no girly mud flaps. Do you understand?"

"Yes, sir."

"I want you to have ten dollars a month just for fun and twenty for your wife. Does that sound fair?"

"Sure do."

"Now, when you get paid, you start at the top of the list. Pay your rent and food categories first. Each time you get more money, add to another category until you get to the bottom of your list. You get the fun money last. Everything extra you put into a fund for your daughter's college. When the month is over, you start over again. Does that seem clear?"

"Clear as a mountain stream!"

"When you're home, don't hang around the house, and for sure don't go to any bars! Start a second business. Can you fix lawn mowers and motorcycles?"

"Son, I could rebuild a diesel engine with a screwdriver and a pair of pliers on a starless night in a tunnel. There's a real good chance I could figure out a lawn mower engine, if I put my mind to it!"

"Great! That's the kind of attitude you'll need before you're through. I know nothing will stop you. The reason nothing will stop you is because you're not going to let it. Your problem is you haven't had any orders from HQ for about twenty years. When your budget says take that hill, you're going to take that hill. Put the word out that you fix mowers. Put your name up here and there in grocery stores, on community bulletin boards, anywhere you can. Work at anything you can while you're home. Anything to keep busy and make a few bucks at the same time. Does that sound like a plan?"

"You better believe it. How can I ever repay you?"

"No, I hope this starts to repay you. I never felt guilty that I didn't serve in the armed services, but I have always felt I owed those who did. I really wonder if I could do the things guys like you did. You may not have volunteered, exactly, but you paid a price. Thank *you*. I appreciate it. Good luck, and keep the faith. You will always be a part of the corps."

Chapter 7
Too Much of a Good Thing

"Say, that was a great seminar! I've heard you speak before, and my wife and I are doing most of what you talked about, but I'm having a little trouble getting my wife on board all the way."

"How is that?"

"Well, I figured out our budget, just like you said, and it has worked real well. We owe nothing on the car and our credit cards, and the house will be paid off about ten years early. The problem is, my wife is still buying things that we don't need!"

"Does she follow the budget? Does she write down every purchase?"

"Yes, but she buys such silly things. We have enough kids' books to stock a library, and she keeps buying little craft things to fill up every nook and cranny in the house!"

"Well, what category does she take it from?"

"She takes it all from what we call Wife."

"So Wife is way in the hole, is that the problem?"

"No, she never gets in the negative area, but she just keeps buying things we don't need."

"Wait a minute. You say she pays for it all out of her exclusive category, and keeps the category in the black. Did I hear you right?"

"Yes, but we don't need all this stuff. We should be

putting it away for something more important, like college or something."

"How much does she get each month; and may I ask you roughly how much do you make, if you don't mind me asking?"

"Wife is one hundred and sixty dollars a month, and I make about fifty thousand dollars a year."

"And how much do you get per month?"

"I get a hundred dollars per month."

"Are the rest of the categories doing okay?"

"Yeah, we get in the red once in a while here and there, but usually it works pretty good."

"Well, I would say she is doing everything just the way I would expect her to. In fact, on your salary I would usually expect her to have more discretionary money, unless you had some big debts or something. As far as living in the spirit of the budget, she is doing just fine."

"But the house is filling up with stuff we don't need!"

"Well, if you need to have a budget for space in the house, that's fine. You know, no kid's books on the kitchen counter, no macrame baskets on the bed. But if her category is of a reasonable size, she buys what is expected of her, like children's clothes, and she keeps within the spending limit, you have no right telling her how to spend her money."

"But she's just wasting it!"

"It doesn't matter if she cuts it up and flushes it down the toilet! It's *her* money. You see, everybody needs a little release from structure. It's the grease that keeps the machine from seizing up. Everybody has to let off a little steam. Not too much steam. If a steam engine lets off too much steam, there isn't enough pressure to make the engine go anywhere. But if you don't let off a little steam, the engine will explode! Only your wife knows what she really wants. Let her spend a little money, however she wants, as long as she follows the rules.

"When you get home after work, don't you like to sit down for a few minutes to relax before dinner? Maybe read the paper, or watch the news?"

"Sure!"

"And if you did it all day, every day, she would have every right to dump you and marry somebody who could hold a job, right?"

"Well, I guess."

"Figure out a way to work out the accumulation problem the same way you work on the budget. You know, the garage is yours, and the kitchen is hers, or vice-versa. Whatever she can't fit in her space has to go. But leave her money category alone! Does that make sense?"

"Yeah, I guess it does. Now that you explain it that way, I guess it does."

"Have you ever had a boss who was a micro-manager?"

"Okay, okay, I get your point!"

"Ah, I can see you have! Well, just keep that in mind."

"I will. Thanks a lot."

"No problem. Good luck."

Chapter 8
A Little Here, a Little There

I guess it's about time I make a confession. I'm not the world-famous financial counselor it may appear. The reason that the name, Steve Johnson, seems so hauntingly familiar is not that I'm famous. No, the reason it sounds like you have heard it before is that it is a collection of a couple of the most common names in America. They're even arranged according to the usual custom of having the first name first and the last name last. Yes, and I have probably only counseled or taught about two hundred people in my life.

No, the last three chapters actually happened only in my imagination. But my experience has told me that, although each person is different, our personalities and weaknesses are not as unique as we might think. Although the caricatures I just described are bigger than life, they aren't pure fiction. If you think about the situations I just described, probably at least one of them applies to you to some degree. In fact, you probably know at least one person who would be similar to each of the persons I just described, but not quite so outlandish.

Furthermore, the ways to success are few and well known. There really aren't that many deep dark secrets, but sometimes we have to look at the world in a little different light. If you do, then the obstacles will take care of themselves. What I am proposing is much more than just adding a budget to the list of things you should do. I am proposing that, if you really want to be successful, you change the way you think.

You don't have to change completely if you don't want to. No doubt you're not as drifty as the surfer, but maybe you're not yet willing to follow a serious budget, either. Do what you can! It's better than nothing. Like the surfer, you will be better off if you change a little, rather than not at all. However, if you declare war on financial troubles, like the cowboy truck driver, there is no reasonable financial goal you can't achieve. The world better step aside for the man or woman who sets his or her mind on a goal and goes after it like a junkyard dog after a juicy steak. While you do this, never let the making of money become the goal. Money is only what you need in order to get where you want to be. For heaven's sake, don't sacrifice what is most important to you for money. You can't take it with you when you die.

When you keep a budget, it forces you to make decisions using a very specific format. Every dollar has a very specific use. Even without a budget, every time you make a purchase you make a decision. But do you evaluate your total financial situation every time you buy something? Do you stop and think when you buy ice cream at the store that this money might otherwise have been spent on a new car? When you go to a movie, do you think, *this money could have been spent on the kids' braces?* When you buy carpet, do you think how many times you could have taken the kids to the community swimming pool for the difference in price between the more expensive carpet and the cheaper one?

When you live by a budget, you sit down and decide how much of your income will be spent on each aspect of your life. How else can you ever plan your finances other than by looking at the big picture? And the big picture is much clearer some Saturday night at home discussing things with your spouse over the kitchen table after the kids are in bed than it is in a big store with some shiny new thing yelling "Buy Me!" at the top of its imaginary lungs. When you budget, you decide how much of your income will go for food, how much for vacation, how much for car maintenance, and how much for retirement.

When you don't budget, you still make the same decisions, except you have no idea how each decision will affect the eventual outcome. It's like someone lost in a dark forest without a compass or a map. Each fork in the path is a guess. You have no idea which path to choose to take you home. Either way, with or without a budget, the decision is still yours; nobody will make it for you. But, if you use a budget wisely, you will cut out a lot of things that are less important to you in favor of other things that are more important.

So, what are some of the things you are going to give up? If you are buying it now, it must be something you want, right? Let me tell you some of the ways our family, or people I know, have saved money.

Let's suppose you buy a soft drink twice a day while at work. Suppose that soft drink cost 65¢ per can out of a machine in the hall. Big deal! What is a buck thirty per day? You owe it to yourself to live a little! I agree, a little treat now and then makes life a lot more pleasant. However, suppose you decided to drink water from the cooler down the hall, which costs nothing, instead of buying two cans of pop each day.

Consider this. There are about fifty weeks in a work year and five work days in a work week. That totals to two hundred and fifty work days per work year. Multiply $1.30 times two hundred and fifty days and you have $325 in a year. That happens to be the exact amount I paid for a good used high-powered sporting rifle and scope. You could buy a very nice sewing machine for that much money. How about a comfy chair for the TV room? Does the kitchen need a new floor? What if the car needed a new clutch; that would about cover it, or at least most of it. Nickels and dimes *do* add up.

I'm not trying to say you shouldn't ever buy a soft drink. If that's what you want, buy it. If sodas are what you really want, buy two six packs for $2.98 and pocket the other $3.52 for other, more important purchases. But don't kid yourself into thinking it's a trivial purchase. Any purchase, no matter how small, becomes significant if it is repeated often enough. The fictitious character of Gulliver was held down by dozens of tiny threads, any one of which he could break with a single finger. If you want it, budget for it. But never forget that you are giving up something else to make that purchase. You will be surprised how much you can save a nickel at a time.

Sometimes saving money requires no change in life-style at all, only a change in how you do things. I use old bread sacks to take my lunch to work, instead of store-bought plastic sacks. What's the difference? They're both plastic. The difference is, one costs money and the other is free. There is another way of looking at this that adds to the social accept-ability of being fiscally responsible. It used to be that unless you were a conspicuous consumer, you were considered a little un-American. Now, when someone gives you a funny little look for using something twice, just smile and say you're being Green. It never made sense to throw perfectly good merchandise in the trash, and it still doesn't! My wife sometimes reuses wrapping paper for presents. We line our wastepaper baskets with the paper or plastic sacks the store gives us for our merchandise. Why buy them in the store when they give them away for free?

My wife and her friends have made a fine art of passing clothes down as the children outgrow them. Kids grow out of clothes so fast sometimes that if you bought all their clothes new, you would go bankrupt. With this network, it seems almost as if no one ever buys any new clothes. Actually they do, but only a fraction of the clothes they might have otherwise. Garage sales, and trips to the thrift shop, further cut the cost tremendously.

Coupons can be a great way to reduce your cost of living. However, be careful. Coupons are usually for more expensive items, which you would otherwise not likely buy. When was the last time you saw a coupon for flour or sugar? Don't be like the guy who bought a jumbo-size bag of dog food, then had to get a dog to eat it. Make sure you're not actually paying more than you would if you had never seen the coupon.

I haven't paid for a hair cut in twenty years. My wife cuts my hair, and does a very fine job. In turn I cut my wife's hair, and often my daughter's also. My only complaint is that lately I have wished my wife would cut my hair a little thicker on top. Her response to this criticism is that she *would* cut it a little thicker, if only I would grow it a little thicker. Oh, well.

Remember how your mother used to tell you to eat your vegetables? That was really good advice, and for more reasons than you may think. Next time you go to the store, compare the price of ten pounds of potatoes and ten pounds of potato chips. Compare the price of a cantaloupe in season with the price of a couple of boxes of your favorite cookies. Not only are fresh fruits and vegetables good healthy foods, they're cheap. Fresh carrots are almost free. So are a lot of other fresh vegetables in the right season. I wouldn't recommend a diet of packaged macaroni and cheese to save money, but I do recommend you stay away from frozen lasagna and takeout Chinese. Food is considerably more expensive when you eat out. Even cheap fast food is a lot more expensive—to say nothing of the nutritional quality—when compared to homemade meals.

Am I trying to say you should not splurge occasionally? No. There is nothing I like better than a small bowl of Rocky Road ice cream in the evening. If I do it once in a while, it won't cost very much, and I won't get all that fat, either. But if I am trying to make ends meet, *something* has to go, and it might as well be in the areas I should be improving, anyway. If you look at the statistics that have been published lately, America needs to watch its weight, as well as its pocketbook. Many people claim they can't cut from their food bill without suffering from a less nutritious diet. That may be for some people, but I think it is usually the other way around.

If you really want to improve your diet, and save money at the same time, try this: Fix cooked oats or some other cooked cereal for breakfast most mornings. If you really want to save money, buy whole wheat and crack it. Mixed with honey, raisins, and cinnamon, it's really very good. Compare that to Sugar Frosted Cocoa Stars for nutrition and price. There wouldn't be so many overweight little kids in America, or parents, for that matter, if we all switched to healthier breakfasts. It may only be a couple of bucks difference—but as I said before, pennies add up.

One gaping hole in many families' finances is electronic entertainment. Count up the number of CDs, audio tapes, video tapes, and the like around your house. Figure out how much you spent on music and movies over the last few years. Is it really worth it? Perhaps the worst abusers are people who get suckered into membership clubs. Book clubs can also be expensive. If you are a member of a club, do yourself a favor and cancel, *right now*. On the other hand, a good book once in a while is a great way to find recreation for a very small price—especially if someone lent you the book, you bought it used, or you took it out of the library.

Have you ever been amazed at the number of "necessities" that have been invented since the year 1960? How did people *live* without a microwave, a VCR, a million battery-powered toys, or, heaven forbid, a computer! For the last four years a friend of mine has priced a computer, gasped at the storage capacity of the disk, calculated the available RAM, and marveled at the latest clock speed. Each year he presents his findings to his wife and exclaims, with a little twinkle in his eye, "—and, Dear, it's almost twice as fast as the one we looked at last year!" She inevitably asks him one simple question: "Explain to me one more time why we need a computer."

The fact is, they don't need a computer, and he knows it. He also has the good common sense to admit it to himself. To date they have yet to buy that computer. No doubt they *will* buy a computer some day, and when they do it will probably be a million times more powerful than all the computers in the world the day Neil Armstrong set foot on the moon. With it they will write letters, concoct spreadsheets, and blast alien invaders like nobody's business. But, in the meantime, more important things will be bought instead.

What are you buying that really isn't that important? Look around. Only you know, and only you know what your priorities should be. This isn't an exhaustive list by any means, but it is a start. Maybe you spend too much on gardening. Maybe you take too many trips. Maybe you have an expensive hobby you could live without. Maybe you are spending too much on gifts for friends. Start setting your priorities right now. Figure out what is most important to you, and begin to formulate a plan to get there.

This reminds me of the time the Cookie Monster was on *Let's Make a Deal* with Monty Hall. The Cookie Monster had made his way to the final round and finally got his chance at the three curtains.

Monty turned to the creature and said, "Now, Cookie

Monster, you get to choose between curtain number one, curtain number two, or curtain number three. To make this even more interesting, I'm going to let you see what is behind each of these three curtains. Behind curtain number one is a new house worth $150,000 next year. Behind curtain number two is a new car worth $30,000 next month. And behind curtain number three is a plate of cookies right now! Okay, Cookie Monster, you have ten seconds to talk it over with your family. Start deciding!"

The camera zooms in on Cookie Monster as he growls in delight with his wife and monster kids until the bell rings and Monty asks, "Okay, Cookie Monster, what is it going to be? The house next year, the car next month, or the cookies *right now!*"

"COOKIE!"

Chapter 9
Plant a Good Seed

I think the most irresponsible thing a parent can possibly do is tell their little children it is fun to play Russian roulette and then leave out a pistol and ammunition to play with. The second most irresponsible thing a parent can do is tell their kids that everybody ought to try drugs at least once, to find out for themselves what drugs are like. The third most irresponsible thing a parent can possibly do is create the illusion for their children that their parents will buy them anything they want.

Fortunately, the first two "crimes against humanity" described above receive the social consternation they deserve. Amazingly, the third seems to be considered normal, if not downright admirable. The social stigma laid against parents who try to teach their kids that money doesn't grow on trees is baffling. The only way you will be able to win against the propaganda onslaught is to recognize it for what it is—the surest way to produce selfish, self-centered brats—and fight it with every determination of your soul.

Now, I'm not trying to suggest for one moment that you shouldn't spend money on your kids. At this point in my life, raising my children is my number one goal. I am willing to make any sacrifice necessary for their development and protection. I have seen some kids shuffle into the supermarket with runny noses, dirty clothes, and no shoes. They look like they escaped from a Charles Dickens novel. I don't know the parents of these unfortunate little ones, but I'm afraid I have very little patience for parents who don't care enough to provide the basic necessities of good hygiene to their children, regardless of how little money they may have. That may change when things get tougher, but currently, at least, it still isn't that hard to wash clothes and buy shoes. We spend a considerable amount of money on books and other educational tools so that our children can have the opportunities we feel are important.

On the other hand, I cannot imagine *why* a parent would want to keep their children in total ignorance about how difficult it is to earn money. We have far too many parents who knuckle under to every whimsical request for the most trivial-yet-expensive toy or some other form of entertainment. Never mind, for the moment, what damage this does to your own budget—think of your children. How will they ever survive as parents if they expect their spouse, the government, or the ubiquitous "they" to provide the continual string of luxuries to which they have become accustomed? The answer is, of course, they won't. The divorce rate is staggering, and over half of those who divorce cite money problems as the single most important factor contributing to their divorce.

But it doesn't have to be that way. How old should your children be before you start to teach them to count, or do the alphabet? When my youngest was not much over three, she could count to ten and knew about half of the alphabet song. Before she is five, she will start to learn from her daddy and mommy about money. My older daughter got an allowance before she could count to one hundred. The first concept to teach your children is that there is a limited amount of money. Therefore, they cannot buy everything they take a fancy to.

Have you ever noticed that supermarkets put the candy and gum next to the checkout stand, right where you have to stand for five to ten years waiting to get out of the store? While you are waiting, your children yell and scream that they will die if they don't get some candy. Do you think that is an accident? If there ever was a plot to destroy America, this has to be it.

So what do you do? Well, while they are two or three, you put up with the yelling, but don't give in and buy the candy. Never negotiate with terrorists or two-year olds; it just encourages them. Buy goodies on your terms and give them out at home. Break the habit of instant gratification before it gets ingrained.

At age nine my oldest daughter, Mindy, takes the younger one, Michelle, and looks in the quarter candy dispensers. Mercifully, this separates the badgerer from the badgered. By the time Mindy was about six, when she asked for candy I simply responded, "Where is your money?" She didn't like that answer, but eventually she learned that I was not going to buy her gum with my money. When I asked her if she was willing to use her money, the money she had worked to get, she frequently lost her desire for whatever it was she'd been dying to get a moment before.

At one point she contrived the concept of a short-term loan. "I'll pay you when I get home," she would say. I didn't like it, but occasionally I relented. One time she pulled a fast one on me and conned me into lending her money on collateral she did not have. When I tried to collect and couldn't, I became the most hard-nosed creditor she had ever seen. I feel I taught her a very important lesson while she was still young; the consequences were quite mild, compared to those she could potentially have as an adult.

Later, Mindy would take her money with her almost every time she went to the store. The problem was, she kept running out of money. Eventually, she would start to get her purse, then change her mind because she didn't want to "waste her money." Recently she bought the T-shirt and matching cap of her favorite sports team, and she did it with her own money. She is not, I have to add, usually too particular about taking care of her clothes, but the hat and shirt are a different story altogether. She almost didn't want anybody to touch them for fear of getting fingerprints on them. When we washed the shirt it had to be just so. Obviously, these were *her* clothes. Slowly, she is learning the value of money.

When I was a boy about eight or nine years of age, my father did something that is a good example of what I think parents should occasionally do. My father is a lawyer, and his firm won a big case that had taken years to settle. Now, before you exclaim, "Well, this guy has no business writing a book about budgeting. He obviously never had it all that tough!" hear me out. My father more closely resembles Atticus Finch from the book *To Kill A Mockingbird* than he does anybody you'd see on TV today. Anyway, the small firm he worked for won a settlement, and he got his share.

That night he came home and sat us down in the living room before an old blackboard and started to explain that we had just received a bonus. It was a large sum of money, more than the price of a new car at the time. Suddenly, I thought, *We're rich!* Then he subtracted a sum for the amount we owed on debts we had incurred since the last big settlement. That took a large hunk, but still I felt that we were in good shape, if not as good as it had appeared at first. Then he explained that he had to pay taxes on the income. The bubble hadn't popped, but it was shrinking fast. This continued until, by the time he was finished, there was only a small fraction of the original sum remaining. I have always remembered that event, and I am sure it has helped to prepare me for the real world I live in. I don't suggest you tell your children every-thing about your finances—they have a habit of blabbing. But don't keep them in the dark, either.

More than once my daughter has pointed out some really nice things that other people are enjoying, and strongly suggested that it would be really neat if we had those fun things, too. Often I have responded point-blank, "Mindy, we can't afford that. We will never be able to afford it. If they invite you to enjoy their things with them, that is fine. You should be grateful. Not everyone gets that opportunity. But just remember, Mindy, we simply cannot afford all the nice things there are in this world."

The truth is, we usually *can* afford the thing she is asking for. Sure, we could buy a speed boat, or a cabin in the mountains. All we would have to do is spend the money that is set aside for her college, the next car we will buy some day, and part of my retirement; then we could buy it! We could probably pay cash! The problem is, all that money is already spoken for, and it is being saved for things that we have decided are more important than a boat or a cabin. But even if I had ten million dollars, I would still tell my daughter that we can't have it. It is more important to me that my daughter be happy throughout her life than indulged when she is young. I am not willing to contribute to a rich life-style while she is young, only to have her be miserable when she is older because her husband can't afford it. Being materialistic is not all it's cracked up to be.

If I were the devil and I were trying to do the most damage I could, I would invent Christmas. Not the Christ-mas described in the tales of O. Henry and Charles Dickens, but the Christmas I see all too often around me every year. Parents are being driven to the poorhouse, buying ever-more-expensive toys that will soon be broken, for children who become ever more demanding and selfish. All the more fantastic because it is done under the pretense of being a good parent. What a devilish idea! Just for the fun of it, try making this year into a family holiday instead of an orgy for the retail business.

When I was nineteen years old, I went on a mission to England for two years on behalf of my church. My parents paid for my mission, and it was no easy task for them, I'm sure. The second Christmas I was in England, my father clipped a branch to use as a Christmas tree from the redwood in the back yard, which I had planted some years before. I'm sure my mother and father were cutting a lot of corners to keep me on my mission, and Dad thought this would be a good way to save a few bucks. When my younger brother and sister saw it, one said, "That's terrible!" The other agreed, "It's not even straight! What a lousy tree!"

"Okay. Fine! Christmas is canceled!" my father declared. He then started to take the branch out of the living room.

Suddenly my brother and sister started singing a different carol, so to speak. "You know, now that I look at it, that branch isn't all that crooked," one said. "And you know, in fact, this is really Steve's tree. We are helping to keep Steve on his mission with the money we are saving by not buying a tree. In fact, didn't Steve plant the tree that this branch came from?"

"Yeah, we'll call this Steve's tree! Now that I can see the tree more clearly it's looking better all the time," the other agreed. My dad proceeded to put the tree back where he had been setting it up a few minutes earlier, a smile on his face.

My younger brother and sister talked about that Christmas as being one of their favorites. I doubt if they could remember more than one or two of the presents they received a year or two after they'd received them, but they did remember sacrificing for someone else. Dare to be different. Dare to make memories.

I have to admit that Santa Claus comes to our house, but we have never used credit to buy a single thing for Christmas. One of the things we do is give things, like clothes, which we might have bought for them, anyway. The toys we do buy are modestly priced. Along with the presents is a letter from Santa telling about what happened with his elves, the reindeer, and Santa Mouse. It costs nothing but a little time and imagination, but it adds to the excitement. Somewhere in the letter there is always mention of the real reason for Christmas. One of the things I like best, and so do the kids, is being some of Santa's helpers. Delivering treats to the houses of people we know, without being caught by the recipients, is a real delight. The cost is small and it's a lot of fun.

Can you remember more than three things you received for Christmas as a child? Give them a present they will always remember, and do it all year long: Give them some of your time. Build something with them in the garage out of some scrap wood. Take them camping. Lie out on the back lawn and look up at the stars. Take them with you as you deliver a pie to someone needy. Teach them to sacrifice for someone else. Teach them to love. There is so little of it in the world; you'll find it's the best investment you'll ever make.

Chapter 10
Automania

Cars! I love cars! Every time a new car is about to be intro-duced to the buying public I usually already know all about it from spy photos and articles published in popular maga-zines. I have loved cars since I was a teenager, more than two decades ago. I *love* cars!

Cars are much more than just steel, glass, and paint. They are something to be cherished. I have a bachelor's degree in mechanical engineering; therefore, I have an intrin-sic interest in all mechanical devices. But there is no compari-son between an electric can opener and a car. Even a VCR or a TV, with all their magic, can't begin to compete with the allure of a new car.

The first car I loved, my parents bought during my senior year in high school. It was just the car I thought our family should have. It was a brand new, dark blue, Chevrolet Vega hatchback. A Vega? The Vega and its sister vehicles were undoubtably the worst cars GM built in the last fifty years! But when we bought it, it was brand-new. Oh, I loved that car!

Let's put things into perspective. The Vega was on a par with the competition from the other American car compa-nies. (The Pinto and Gremlin were no works of perfection, either.) There is a good reason the Japanese and Europeans beat up the U.S. carmakers in the seventies and early eighties:

their cars were better. Things have changed a lot in the car business since then. I have to say that they don't make cars like they used to, and I'm glad! And every time they bring out a new car, I fall in love all over again!

So, how many new cars have I bought since I got married over fifteen years ago? I am a mechanical engineer making good money. A car is something my family needs. A car is very useful in America these days. How many new cars have I bought?

None! Not one! Why not? Why do I drive a bunch of junky old cars?

Well, let's set the record straight. I don't drive a bunch of junky old cars. The last car I bought was a four-year-old Buick LeSabre. It looked almost brand-new as I drove it home. The seats were a tiny bit discolored, and there were a couple of places where shopping carts had done their mischief. Other than that, the car looked brand-new. It had seventy thousand miles on the odometer, which is a bit much; but as I test-drove the car, I couldn't tell the difference between it and a new car. It was obvious that whoever owned that car had taken good care of it for the four years that they had it. Three years later it still drives great.

We had seen a similar car earlier in the day at a different dealership, but that car was beat. When I looked under the hood and under the car, I could see obvious signs of a hard life. The salesman mentioned that it wasn't working just yet, but they could have a mechanic on it and it would be running by noon, if we wanted to come back to test drive it after lunch. "Thanks, anyway." I was not about to buy a car they hadn't even managed to patch up long enough for me to test drive.

I had seen a third Buick LeSabre for sale at a repo yard behind the credit union near where I work. It was about the same year, in good shape, but they'd wanted four thousand dollars more than the one I eventually bought.

The reason I bought the car from a dealer, instead of a private citizen as I have in the past, is that it was hard to find a relatively new Buick for sale in the paper. Had I found one in the paper, I would have cut out the middle man and split the difference with the previous owner. However, most people who have nice sedans don't sell them in the paper; they trade them in on a new car, after a few years, or they keep them for life.

The car originally sold for about $18,000 in 1988. Four years later I bought it for about half that price. I have had it for over three years, and I have spent less than $700 total on repairs and maintenance, including replacing a cracked windshield. If the car blows into a million pieces a year from now, I will still have done better than the previous owner in terms of dollars per year. I know that, because I know the dealer charged at least $1,000, probably $2,000 for the bother of keeping the car on his lot for a couple of weeks. Of course, the car won't blow up in a year. It will keep on running for at least another ten. And every year it goes farther, it makes the price per year that much better. All during that time I will be taking care of that car as if it were worth a lot of money.

Notice I keep mentioning the Buick LeSabre. The reason I picked that car is that I had done my homework, and that was the choice at the top of my list of potential cars to buy that particular year. There were other cars that were close contenders, like the Ford Taurus, but I had decided the Buick was my first choice. A few years later and my first choice would not have been the LeSabre. It is important that you keep current and not rest on old data. The Buick LeSabre had a 3.8 liter engine, which is highly acclaimed. I knew that the LeSabre had been rated as one of the safest cars for that model year, and I also wanted front-wheel drive. I also knew that it got excellent gas mileage, about thirty miles to the gallon on the freeway. I knew it would hold my family comfortably on trips and be easy to drive. Most importantly, my wife approved of the way it looked.

When I walked into the dealership and the salesman asked if he could help me, I said, "Yes, I'm looking for a Buick LeSabre with all the gauges, not more than four years old, and I don't want to pay more than $9,000 for it, depending on its condition."

It blew the salesman away. He told me later that when he asks most people what kind of car they are looking for, they respond by saying something like, "I don't know, probably a bigger one. Have you got one in white?" Of course, he always has just the perfect car. In other words, the dealer will sell whatever he happens to have on the lot, and the buyer may never realize what he could have had if he had only studied the market.

It's not like I am an expert on cars. Lots of people know lots more than I do. The problem is, far more know far less. Do your homework! Read about the different cars. Find out how much they cost used. There are books published each year that give you a lot of information on used-car prices. Ask people who own a car like the one you are considering how they like it. Talk to a mechanic. Ask him what kind of car he would buy if he were you, and why. Four or five hours of homework could make a big difference.

So what do I recommend? I recommend that you buy a brand-new car, drive it for about four years, and sell it for less than half what you paid for it. Be sure to get a four-door, with all the gauges; and if you don't mind, please get a light metallic blue or white. While you're at it, would you mind not smoking in my car? I can get rid of the smell, but it takes a little effort. Oh, did I say *my* car? Well, since you're only going to keep it for four years, and I'm going to keep it for at least twelve, it does seem only natural that I should refer to it as mine.

Am I completely happy with the Buick? Well, there is the problem with the gear-shift knob. It fell off while my wife was driving it. No, it wasn't broken off, it fell off. What a piece of junk! I don't know what the problem is; the shifter knob on our '69 Chevy never fell off in the twenty-three years that we owned that car. Whoever used to design shifter knobs at GM must have died. Now they can't do it right anymore. So what did I do? Remember, I have a bachelor of science degree in mechanical engineering: I glued it back on. Yep, one big gob of glue, and it's been there ever since.

It has had a couple of other problems over the last three years, but probably the most aggravating was the time the alternator bearing seized up. When that happened, the alternator housing around the bearing tore apart. Fortunately, I was in town when it happened, so I limped the car home and started to fix it in the driveway. Once I figured out what the problem was, it was merely a matter of removing the serpentine belt, removing three bolts, unclipping the wire cable, getting a rebuilt alternator for a little over $100, and replacing the cable, bolts, and belt. The serpentine belt was a bit tricky until I figured it out, but today I could do the whole operation in under thirty minutes, no sweat.

So why was it aggravating? I'll tell you why it was so aggravating. That bearing should never have failed! The technology is there to make a bearing last a lot more than five years and 75,000 miles. Our '69 Chevy lasted twice as many miles and four times as many years without failing. No doubt it was about to go, but those little bearings were still rolling. And to add insult to injury, the rebuilt alternator cost at least three times as much for a new Buick as an old Chevy alternator would have. Maybe I'm a purist, but that stuck in my craw.

Now look at the other side of the coin. I have heard of people who have had problems that have stranded them in traffic with a car that is less than six months old. Don't tell me that new cars don't have troubles. I know better. The on-board computers are more likely to fail during the burn-in period, which is the first few hundred miles, than at any other time in the life of the car. Oh, sure, you will have an extended warranty. And how much does that cost? When you add the purchase price of the Buick to the repairs I expect to make on my car, I anticipate that my car will cost me about $1,200 per year. Compare that to the previous owner, who paid more like $3,000 per year! I don't mind replacing an alternator in my driveway for $1,800 per year. How about you?

So how do I get my cars to last more than seven years? Doesn't it cost a lot to keep a car going that long? Well, you can start by throwing all that stuff out of the garage that you should never have bought in the first place, and put your car there when you're not driving it. That will go a long way toward making your car look new longer. It helps the battery, and plastic parts last longer as well. Next, do the little things, like changing the oil and filter every three months or 3,000 miles. I don't care if the manual says it will go 7,500 miles; oil changes are a lot cheaper than a new engine. Keep track so you know when one is needed. I keep a log book in every car we own and write down everything about each car. (You probably could have guessed that.)

How long has it been since you had your transmission fluid changed? If you did that every three or four years, along with the filter, your transmission would last almost forever. How about your fuel filter? When was it last changed? When you change the engine coolant every two years, add cooling system lubricant. It costs about a dollar. This will make your water pump last longer as well. A water pump is not that expensive, but it costs a lot more than a dollar, and they are hard to change. A water pump could cost $300 to have a mechanic replace, so it is well worth the preventative maintenance. Read about your car, and treat it as if you plan to keep it for a decade or so. If you do, it will function a lot better and will be more fun to own.

The best way you can make your car last longer is not to drive it. You have to drive it sometimes, of course, but 25,000 miles a year? I put less than 10,000 miles per year on both my cars together, and that includes a couple of trips across four western states each summer. Consolidate or eliminate trips whenever possible. The government gives more than 30¢ per mile to people who drive their own cars on official business. They don't do that because they are generous! They do it because that is about how much it actually costs. Gas is only a fraction of the cost of driving. If you're going to drive a long way to save money, make sure it's a lot of money. If you drive 100 miles to save $30, you just wasted your time.

If you bought a reasonable car in the first place, you should be able to get at least a decade and a half out of your car. Our second car was seven years old when I bought it from a little old lady, who only drove it on Sundays to the racetrack where she smoked cigars. It only had 32,000 miles on it when I bought it for about $2,300. It is currently thirteen years old, and I expect to get at least another five years out of it—ten if I push it, figuratively speaking. If you live somewhere where there are harsh winters, you may have to take this all with a grain of salt, as they say. As you know, salt eats up steel cars. Some recent models have external plastic body parts. That would be a real plus, if you can find one without sacrificing some other feature you need. You may not be able to make your car last as long as I do, living in the desert southwest; but, with a little effort on your part, you can probably do a lot better than most people.

I used to do all my car fixing, and I still do a lot of it myself. I do this for two reasons. First, it is cheaper, of course. Second, have you ever seen those guys who work on cars back in those grease bays? I worked in gas stations to pay my way through college, and I have to say, many of these grease monkeys are not exactly Einsteins. If I don't know exactly what I am doing, I'm at least on a par with a lot of them. I can learn, just like they do. When I get over my head, I go to a mechanic I trust. Once you find a good mechanic, *never* go anywhere else to save a buck. Be nice to him; take him a cake on his birthday. He is worth his weight in gold. In fact, you could buy gold with the money you save from fixing only what needs to be fixed, and fixing it only once.

Even if you are not inclined to do any of the work yourself, you can save money if you know a few things about cars. On one of our trips recently, I hit a dead animal lying in the middle of the freeway. Soon after I began to notice the car didn't idle properly, and it seemed to shift oddly. I worried that maybe the animal had dented the pan in the bottom of the transmission. The symptoms all seemed to indicate that it had.

Finally, when I got a chance to take a good look under the car, sure enough, I could see a place where the pan was dented. As I looked closer I realized that the dent had been made deliberately, produced in the forming process of the pan. It was actually the place where a magnet rests on the opposite side of the pan to collect metal shavings in order to protect the transmission. As I examined the situation more closely I noticed some hair still stuck farther back under the car, which led me to a metal shroud around the exhaust pipe. The shroud was there to protect the bottom of the car from getting too hot from the hot exhaust pipe. The shroud had been bent up against the exhaust pipe as a result of the impact with the animal's body. I took a screwdriver, pried the shroud away from the exhaust pipe, and the problem went away.

Suppose I had taken the car into a transmission shop

without looking under the car. They would have fixed the transmission. When they'd gotten through, and the problem persisted, they would have looked a second time, noticed the shroud, and pried it back. Then they would have charged me $850 and never mentioned the shroud. I would have paid the price and thought, "Gee, they sure did a good job of fixing my car."

Now, stop and think about this a minute before you get mad at the mechanic. What do they do in a transmission shop? Fix transmissions. What did you ask them to do in the transmission shop? Fix the transmission. It doesn't take that much to get a little acquainted with a car and find out what the shocks do, and where the spark plugs go. It's not that hard to flush a radiator. With the right attitude it can even be a little fun, once you realize how much you can do if you just take a little interest in your car.

So what happens if you have a major car problem? Get it fixed. If the transmission blows up, have it rebuilt! Spend the $850 that you saved for such occasions in the car category and be done with it. After all, how often does the transmission blow up? Certainly not every year. If it does, you have one lemon of a car. Even if it did, it's less than the $3,000 per year the previous owner of my Buick paid for every year he or she owned it. Listen for those funny little noises. Often you can fix the problem before it gets out of hand.

Other hidden costs of a new car are the sales tax, registration, and insurance. These are generally based on the purchase price of the car, and two of them have a way of sticking around for a long time. If you buy a car for half as much, the other fees are considerably reduced as well. Also, new cars are more likely to be stolen, all other things being equal. It is not a bad idea to have an older car if you are trying to make yourself a low profile target for crime.

"Yes, but it isn't a new car!" I can hear you say. I told

you I love *new* cars. Well, that is true. But I have it on good authority: Studies have proven over 97 percent of cars purchased new more than two years ago are now at least two years old! New cars aren't new for long. It's a tremendous price to pay for the privilege of being the first person to get the car dirty. I make a hobby of looking at cars that are new with an eye toward the day when I plan to own them used. That gives someone else three or four years to test the car I will own some day so that I don't wind up owning a Vega, like my Dad did. (He still doesn't want to talk about that Vega.)

Why do I make such a big deal about new cars? The reason is simple: New cars cost a bunch of dough! There are a lot of things that can nickel and dime you to death. But when we're talking $15,000 or $25,000 for a new car, we're talking some real bucks! I figure I am saving at least $1,200 per year over the cost of buying the same car new and keeping it for five to seven years. There is a lot I can do with more than $1,200 per year! Another way of looking at it is: I am buying a much better car used than if it were a cheap little new car. Either way you look at it, you win.

Of course, I never buy a car on credit. (Believe it or not, they will take a check.) The interest on a car loan is enough to save for a kid's college, or for your own retirement. Interest on a car loan amounts to hundreds of dollars per year. Don't throw it away on impatience. Make regular car payments to the Car category, and voilà, the money is there when you need it. Pay the interest to yourself. Don't tell me you can't afford to save for a car. If you can't afford to do that, then you can't afford a car. When do you ever expect to get ahead of the game, if not now?

There is another reason for keeping the same car for at least a decade that is very compelling, at least to me. At a plastics seminar I attended recently, in line with my profession, I noticed the hot topic was recyclability. Increasingly, more of every car is made of plastic. Making these parts recyclable is a very difficult but important problem for the car industry. There are two ways of reducing the solid waste problem. One is to make a product that can easily be disassembled, sorted, reground, and remolded, using some fraction of new material, into a new product. Second, you can simply make the product last longer. If you keep a product twice as long before you throw it away, the landfill will be half as full.

I propose that, short of an accident, most cars go to the dump with the majority of their parts still functional. Many cars, had they been properly taken care of, could be driven many more miles before they are junked. The problem is, it doesn't take many things going wrong before a car doesn't work at all. This is not all the fault of the carmakers, although they bear their share of guilt. We should do our part as well.

Obviously, cars do eventually wear out; but the landfill problem could be cut in half if *we* made our cars last twice as long. I am not an environmentalist, by any means, but I do agree with them when it comes to treating the resources of the world as if they were Kleenex. A car is not a Kleenex. Treat your car as if it is something of value, and it will be for many, many years. We need that landfill space for something else; and you need the money you will save for something else, as well.

I love new cars! I really do! I just don't love them twice as much as the ones that were new four years ago.

Chapter 11
A House Could Be a Home

Let me tell you how to make a million dollars in real estate. Start by buying the biggest house you can, at the best price, for the lowest down payment, using equity from a home loan and a little loan from your brother in Phoenix. Rent the house at the highest rate the market will bear. After a few years, when the house has appreciated thirty percent, sell it and buy three more homes with the equity, which has tripled. Repeat this process over and over until you have $1,000,000. People in real estate call this leverage. It is also called Russian roulette!

Now let me tell you how to *lose* three million dollars (which you don't have) in real estate. Start by buying the biggest house you can, at the best price, for the lowest down payment, using equity from a home loan and a little loan from your brother in Phoenix. Rent the house at the highest rate the market will bear. After a few years, when the house has appreciated thirty percent, sell it and buy three more homes with the equity, which has tripled. Repeat this process over and over until you are about to make $1,000,000. At this point the aerospace industry, or oil boom, or whatever it was that over-inflated the price of real estate to begin with, goes bust. You are then left with a bunch of houses that aren't worth what you paid for them, and no one to rent them to.

Next, you leave town and never show your face anywhere near Phoenix.

The concept of leverage is very simple. If you can borrow money at one rate and invest it at a higher rate, you make money. How much you can make is limited only by how much you can borrow. If you borrow $1,000 at 5 percent and reinvest it at 10 percent, you will make $50 in one year. If, instead, you borrow $1,000,000 using the same scheme, you will make $50,000 in that same year. The problem is this: The reason the rate of return is greater on one investment than on another is usually because the risk is correspondingly greater. If that were not true, the lender would invest it at the higher rate and leave you out. If you borrow $1,000,000 and the investment loses 10 percent, you now owe the bank $1,050,000, and you have $900,000. You somehow have to make up the difference or go into default. Yes, there are several people who are famous because they made a lot of money in a very short period of time. There are a lot more who aren't famous, who lost everything they had and more.

There are at least two ways of thinking about a house. One is to think of it as an investment. That is a useful way to think of it, and I will use that concept later, but for the moment I want you to think of it as a basic commodity of life. You will die without oxygen in a matter of minutes. Fortunately, air is still free. You will die without water in a week. Water isn't free, but you won't ever drink enough to go broke. You will die in a month or two without food, but food can easily cost less than a hundred dollars a month per person, with the exception of teenage boys—the modern equivalent of the biblical plague of locusts. There are many places in the United States where you can live almost all year long without a roof over your head if you have a reasonably good sleeping bag. However, most people in the United States would not find this an acceptable arrangement.

A house provides three things: First, it protects us from the elements. Second, it provides a place for us to exist; there are not many places you are welcome unless you pay. Third, a house provides a place to keep all the things you want to have. We are not bedouins, most of us, anyway. If we were, a microbus with hand-painted flowers all over it would do fine. If you find the option of living in the back of a station wagon absolutely unacceptable, then you should act like it is absolutely unacceptable!

It matters little to me whether the price of our house rises or falls. My house is not an investment; it's where I live. I can't sell my house without buying another one, because we refuse to live without a house.

How much would you take in exchange for a seat on a plane? What if it was 1975 in Saigon and you had worked in military intelligence for the South Vietnamese government, and this was the last plane leaving before the Communists arrive? Would you sell a vest? What if it was a life vest and the *Titanic* had just gone down? Would you trade it for stocks? How about government bonds? If your house is so important that you can't imagine living without it, then pay for it and keep it!

Whether the price of my house inflates to $500,000 or drops to $5,000 doesn't matter to me. It still has the same number of rooms. It still has a sink in the kitchen. It still has a garage that fits two cars. No matter what the price of the house, we still have to live somewhere. Whether there is hyperinflation or a catastrophic depression, as long as I can hold onto my home I don't care how many dollars the market assigns to its value.

Some "experts" provide a compelling argument that, under certain economic conditions, you are better off renting and investing your money somewhere else. Although this may work under certain conditions, I generally consider this to be sheer folly. A house is one of the few investments a common person can make that has actual intrinsic value. What is money? Money is paper with ink on both sides. We all agree it represents something else of value, but that could change. Can you eat money? Can you drink corporate bonds? Will stocks keep the rain off or the wind out? If you own your own home, pay the taxes on your house, and buy food, you can get by, no matter how bad things get. If, through some major stroke of luck, everything goes just fine for the rest of your life, don't feel bad. You can still leave a nice estate to your children.

Remember earlier in chapter 2, I mentioned that paying off a loan is better than investing at the same interest rate? The same is true of a home loan, only more so. Protect the investment in your house to the bitter end. If you lost your house, where would you go? Where would you live?

There is a significant exception to this philosophy. If you move every two or three years because you are in the military service, or because you have some other job that requires you to move, you will lose too much on the cost of selling a home to make home ownership worth it. Generally, the cost to buy and sell a home is at least 8 percent of the value of the house. It just doesn't make sense, if you move often, to buy a house everywhere you move. Find some other investment. Maybe an option is to buy a house somewhere, perhaps in the town where you plan to retire, and rent it out until you need it. You can even buy a different house when you retire. Just be sure you own the deed to some property, somewhere.

When you are older, if all else fails, you can borrow against the equity in your house to live on. This is when you start to think of your house as an investment. The more money you have invested in your home, presumably, the more you have to take out of it. The fact that it is a tangible asset, rather than an abstraction, is something not normally thought about, but it may become very important someday.

If there is a nationwide depression, the price of your home will plummet, but so will the price of everything else. In other words, your house may drop in price from, say, $150,000 to $10,000, but so will the price of most other things. Unfortunately, not only will the price of most things drop in a depression, but probably so will your income. You may need all the available money from whatever meager income you earn just to put food on the table. A house payment will loom ever larger if your salary is reduced as a result of a depression.

If there is hyperinflation the price of your home will soar, but again so will the price of everything else. In this case, you make out like a bandit on the sales price of your house, and every other purchase you still owe money on, but you lose on everything else. This causes panic buying until something forces it to stop, or the economy collapses.

The money you make on the inflation of the price of your house is only an illusion. In fact, what is really happening during hyperinflation is money is becoming worthless. Your house is not really worth more each day. There are the same number of rooms, and the garage is the same size. It just takes more and more money to buy a house, so in real terms the money is becoming less and less valuable. Again, what is important are your tangible assets.

The fact that the debt on your home would be diminished into insignificance is precisely why I don't think hyperinflation is likely to happen soon. If you assume that the rich lend the most money, and are the ones who most influence government and control the economy, you would also have to assume that they would try very hard to prevent hyperinflation. They would do this because they have the most to lose. It seems unlikely to me that they would allow hyperinflation if they can possibly prevent it, because it hurts them to have the companies they own go broke and their money become worthless.

However, inflation doesn't just happen—it is *caused*. When a government prints money much faster than the increase in goods and services, inflation occurs. If that happens, it means you and everyone else will be hurt. Fortunes will be wiped out overnight. I tend to believe the theory that the rich like to get richer. However, I believe that sometimes bad things happen that aren't planned.

Why do I keep talking like the stock market could crash some day, or the government could start defaulting on its loans, or a massive earthquake in California could cause half a trillion dollars worth of damage that would wreck the economy, or a civil war in the former Soviet Union could boil over into Europe, or as if massive civil unrest is possible in the United States? If you look at history, I think you will find that the last few decades have been unusually calm in terms of the impact of world events on the United States.

Suppose you are born in 1900. When you are six years old San Francisco first shakes, then burns to the ground in the great quake of 1906. You're a bit young; besides, you don't live in California, so it isn't a problem for you. When you are fourteen Europe goes to war. That doesn't matter either, because you live in the United States. In 1918 it suddenly does matter, because you get drafted and sent to France to fight. Fortunately, you don't see much action and come home with some spiffy stories to tell. You marry in 1921 while in college. Your first baby comes in 1923, a son. You find a good job in a car design facility that same year. Your second child comes in 1925. In 1926 you move to your own home. You really have to stretch—but wow, a house of your own! Your third child comes in the fall of 1928. You move into the position of supervisor over your section and have ten people working for you. You really have it made!

Speculation is the modern way to make money, and the quick profits are there for the taking. You scrape together a hundred dollars and leverage it to four hundred. There seems no end to the possibilities. You could make a thousand dollars by 1930!

In October 1929 the bottom falls out of the stock market! By 1931, as the plant closes its doors, you are the last person in the section you used to supervise. A wife, three children, and no job! Losing your job was bad enough, but losing your house is devastating. The irony—that you only get fifteen cents on the dollar for what little money you had in the bank, yet the home loan is still dollar for dollar—is absolutely galling.

The night you lose your home you stand there in the hot summer air, tears rolling down your cheeks, telling your father that you are a failure. He reminds you of your grandfather, who lost his house in the Civil War. Your great-grandfather lost three farms to bad crops. You did the best you could, but sometimes that just isn't good enough. His words are comforting but not convincing.

You look for work all over the Great Lakes area; finally, you give up and move to Los Angeles to live with your brother-in-law. The plan is to stay just long enough to find steady work. Your brother-in-law's salary was cut, and what you make at odd jobs helps pay his mortgage. You're still looking for steady work when the Long Beach earthquake hits in 1933. The quake is moderate, but because of poor building standards the damage is extensive. For you the Long Beach quake turns out to be a blessing in disguise, because you find work rebuilding the damaged city.

Eventually you land a job with the city of Los Angeles, as the Great Depression slowly grinds on into its fourth year.

Later in 1934 you move into your own apartment. The two and a half years you spent with your in-laws were hard, but later you will reminisce about those times as "the good old days." Things keep picking up as the thirties come to a close, but there is a familiar sound in Europe, and you don't like the sound of it. Your oldest, Frank, approaches draft age. In 1938, you buy another house. In 1939, Hitler invades Poland. America is still safe, since America has no wish to become embroiled in a war that is none of its concern.

December 7, 1941: Japan bombs Pearl Harbor; Frank is almost 19 years old. He is gone in six months, and America stops everything to mobilize for war with virtually every available resource. Car production for civilian use virtually stops. Every nonessential commodity—refrigerators, washers, everything possible—is put on hold for four years while the world is made safe from fascism.

The war is a mixed blessing for America. The depression finally fades away unnoticed as the country arms itself for war, but the war claims the lives of over 400,000 of America's finest. The rest of the world is far less fortunate. Europe and the Far East are destroyed, taking over fifty million casualties. The war ends in two blinding flashes of light. Frank is one of the lucky ones—he comes home in one piece. Predictions of a return to depression circulate widely. They prove to be unfounded, as the pent-up demand of millions trying to make up for lost time pushes the economy forward. The revved up economy and gutting of the military budget help to pay a major portion of the huge war debt. America is finally reaching a level of prosperity you haven't seen since 1929, almost twenty years before. The future really looks bright as your fiftieth birthday rolls around, until June 1950.

A massive invasion of South Korea by North Korea once again plunges America into a war it neither wants nor is prepared for. Five years after beating simultaneously both the Nazi military machine and imperial Japan, America is unable to stop the onslaught of a Third World country without committing a huge portion of its military. Panic buying grips America, as fears of World War III sweep the country. Frank, who stayed in the Army National Guard, is called up and goes to war again; but this time he is not so lucky. He returns with his right arm and sight missing. Fortunately, as a veteran he receives benefits, but the personal toll is something Frank never fully recovers from.

The Korean War ends in 1953, and life returns to more civil pursuits. The cold war is real, but eventually seems to fade from view due to overexposure. Other pursuits occupy the public mind as the fifties move on. You pay off the balance of your home loan, retire, and start a business of your own at age sixty-two. You're a little baffled by the world you see around you. The financial security you have worked your whole life to obtain becomes less important to the youth around you, who have never had to go without. They just aren't impressed by what you have managed to scratch out in a lifetime. In years gone by, a party would have been given to celebrate the burning of the mortgage. Few people seem to care anymore. Suddenly the world hangs in the balance, as Kennedy and Khrushchev go up to the edge of Armageddon over missiles in Cuba. The crisis is over as fast as it starts, but then there is this nagging war in Vietnam which won't go away.

In 1963, the President is killed in broad daylight. Vice President Lyndon Johnson is sworn in, and with the mantle of authority come apparently insoluble problems. Johnson declares war on poverty but never declares war in Vietnam, even though the number of troops grows to half a million in the country. The Watts riots tear Los Angeles apart before your eyes, and some wonder how it will all end. President Johnson resolves the dilemma of how to pay for guns and butter by paying for both with borrowed money. Entitlements are expanded, but they are only a small fraction of government spending, and are projected to stay that way for decades.

By the end of the sixties the war and civil disorder bring you things you could never have imagined. Black Panthers claim they will declare war on whites if Huey Newton is convicted of murder. The Weathermen Underground rob banks to finance their effort to overthrow the federal government. At Kent State, youths are shot down on campus by National Guard soldiers; color TV shows you pictures of U. S. servicemen sitting in a circle sharing a pipe of hashish. This isn't the army you remember. You retire a final time at age sixty-nine.

You turn seventy and the world gets crazier. In 1972, Richard Nixon wins the presidential election but ends up resigning from office. Your investments start to lose their luster as inflation heats up. The company retirement and social security just don't keep up with the faster and faster rate of inflation. The seventies end none too soon with simultaneous stagnation and inflation, which is dubbed "stagflation." The eighties start by replacing stagflation with a serious depression. This is nothing compared to the Great Depression, but is certainly serious enough for the millions of unemployed. You breathe a sigh of relief, because the inflation that was eating away at your savings and investments has finally abated. The year 1984 comes around and you look back on a long and full life. Your wife is still spry and takes care of both your needs and Frank's, but you have a hard time making it out of the chair anymore. The year 1987 comes and you look back and wonder if the world doesn't look just a little bit like it did sixty years ago: young, restless, out for a good time, no care for tomorrow. Maybe not; maybe the future will be different.

What am I trying to say? Am I trying to suggest that the stock market crash of 1929 and WW II are about to be repeated? Certainly not. But calamities do happen. This century has had more disaster than tranquility, and we should expect more of the same. I really haven't the foggiest clue as to what specifically will happen in the future. However, I know what a freight train sounds like when it is coming just around the corner, and I want to get off the tracks before it gets here. I don't know when it will happen, or what form it will take, but I think massive debt on the part of individuals, corporations, and particularly governments, including foreign governments, will bring about an extended period of severe hardship in America. I think large numbers of people will go hungry for the first time in their lives.

Maybe your home will be destroyed, as in Sherman's March to the Sea, or burned to the ground, as in the San Francisco earthquake. If that is the case, my advice didn't help you very much. But before you disregard my advice, talk to the farmers who lost their farms in the 1980s because they took on too much debt. Ask them how well the government protected them. Ask yourself whether it couldn't have been avoided. Ask yourself whether it could happen to you.

Some people claim you should either own your house outright or be as far mortgaged as possible. The rationale is that the houses that are almost paid for will be the first to be repossessed. The argument is sound. The problem is, there is no way to get from here to there without being somewhere in between. How would someone go about saving enough to pay for their house in one giant payment? Be cautious, but not fatalistic. Life does go on.

Another argument goes like this: "What's the use? No matter what you do, when it all crashes down anything you might have will be stolen or burned by the marauding bands of thieves. What you *really* need is a bunker and an assault rifle." This argument doesn't allow for anything in the middle. It's either happy land or death and destruction. Most scenarios fall in between these two extremes. People still went to college in the thirties. People still bought houses in World War II. Hard times don't have to be the end of the world, and you can improve your ability to cope with them if you act prudently.

So, buy yourself a house, if you can. Look at the neighborhood and make sure it has good resale. Remember the three most important things about buying a house are location, location, and location. Don't overextend! Fix the house up the way you like it. Plant some trees in the yard. Have a barbecue. Enjoy your house. And start paying it off in a systematic, methodical fashion, and do it in less than the maximum time. If you start early, you can pay off your house in half the time with a modest increase in payment each month.

Let's suppose I'm all wet. Maybe the next fifty years will be just great; anything is possible. So, leave your children a nice little inheritance, just when they need it most. Why do you have to die broke? But if I'm right, you may discover what Scarlett O'Hara realized after the Civil War, during Reconstruction. After your family, the most important thing in your life is the dirt that you own and live on, your Tara.

Chapter 12
Squirrels Do It

The last chapter was intended to emphasize the concept of doing first things first. Having the necessities of life secured ought to be your first objective, but not your only one. Now I'm going to give you a broad perspective of investments to consider that includes your house, among other things. Once you have home base relatively secure, you can do some very interesting things with money other than spend it.

Let's start by talking about savings. Go to your favorite discount store sometime, and when you reach the checkout stand, tell the salesperson that you would like to withdraw fifty dollars. When they give you a funny look, explain to them that you have been saving at this store for years, and now you would like to withdraw some of your savings. At this point they will probably call for the manager, who will kindly escort you out.

Spending isn't saving! The whole idea of saving and investing is to postpone buying something now in the hope of having something more important later. Squirrels do this every summer. The story of the grasshopper that fiddled while the ants worked also comes to mind. For thousands of years mankind generally has prepared for the future. In Oriental cultures, it is typical to think of saving for the future in terms of generations. Modern Americans seem to disdain such thoughts. The average American spends 97 percent of what he or she earns. The Japanese and Germans save about two to three times as much as we do. I make a big distinction between savings and investments. Savings is whatever you can liquidate quickly without a penalty. This includes bank accounts, checking accounts, money under the mattress, short-term fixed interest deposits, and so forth. Investments are what you have to sit on, sometimes for decades, to see the expected reward. This includes stocks, bonds, land, children, and so on. For me, decades means age sixty. I plan on living at least fifteen years past age sixty, and my wife will probably live another ten years past that. If you're investing for retirement, or a college fund, decades is not too long.

Suppose you were to have deposited $10,000 into a mutual fund, which was designed to match exactly the Standard and Poor's 500 Index on June 30, 1985. That investment would have grown to $32,127 by October 31, 1993, just over eight years later. That happens to be an annual rate of increase of 15.0 percent. I found those numbers in an annual report printed by the Vanguard Group, one of the largest families of mutual funds in the United States. Fifteen percent is above the historical average of the stock market, which has been about 10 percent per year, but I think it makes my point. Since the Standard and Poor's is an average of sorts, some stocks did better and some did worse. Think about it for a while. You don't have to spend all your money; you could put some of it to work for you.

As I mentioned, the stock market has risen more than 10 per cent per year during the years between 1926 to 1990. That includes the stock market crash of 1929 and several other dramatic downturns, such as the one that occurred in October 1987. If that sixty-four-year stretch of history is an indication of the future, and if you are willing to stick it out, you have a very good chance of doing very well by investing in stocks. Of course, I'm not saying you *absolutely* will, but you might.

If you invest for one year, you have a 24 percent chance of losing part of your original investment and a 19 percent chance of making 10 to 20 percent increase. That doesn't sound too good, does it? If you stay in for twenty years, you have a 0 percent chance of losing part of your original investment, and a 70 percent chance of receiving 10 to 20 percent return. Now that sounds much more appealing! Those probabilities are based on the same historical sixty-four-year time period mentioned above. The chance for a return on your investment is very real, but you have to know the rules of the game, or you could lose your shirt.

I'm going to list a series of investments, starting with the most secure and working toward the wild side. My strongest recommendation is that you start at the most secure end of the investment spectrum until you have your essentials secured, then work your way toward the more risky side. If you jump in at the deep end first, you could drown.

In my opinion, the most secure investment you can make is to give to the charity of your choice. Regardless of whatever may happen, you need to pay your dues. Many people accept this as a commandment resulting from their religious convictions. Others simply observe that they are part of the human race. Every one of us owes a debt to others we can never repay. No matter how little you have, or how little you can afford to give, if you give of yourself you will be a richer person for so doing. Don't be a Scrooge!

The very next investment I would make is in food. Even if it's only $50 worth of canned goods and a flashlight stored by the garage door in case of an earthquake, hurricane, or blizzard, it's a start. Food is a terrific investment for a tiny bit of money. As you get more established, you can invest more in food until you have enough to subsist on for months, even a year or more. This assumes you have at least a little income, perhaps a small garden, to supplement your food storage with bits of fresh food. There are many people who have lived off their food storage for extended periods of time, and you could, too. This will come in handy if you are laid off from a job, or even if, heaven forbid, some massive disaster hits you along with many others.

What I'm suggesting is wheat, beans, rice, sugar, or honey, rolled oats, and things like that, all properly sealed in plastic or metal containers. Add to that some cases of canned soups, stews, tuna, fruit, vegetables, peanut butter, honey, and vegetable oil. Be sure to store these properly and rotate them, or else you may find the weevils beat you to the punch when you finally need them. String beans and tomato paste are very acidic and don't last long in a can, so stay away from them. Storing food isn't that difficult (finding the space might be harder); and when you find out what real homemade bread tastes like, you may not want to eat that store-bought stuff any more. If you use some of these bulk items in your diet, you should soon find a reduction in your food budget and very possibly an improvement in your health. It takes effort, but who said life was easy? I suggest you visit your library, bookstore, or health-food store to learn more about food storage.

The next investment I would suggest is to buy a house. This will take much longer to pay for than a year's worth of food, but it is almost as important. Since the last chapter was devoted to the subject of home ownership, I will add only one more thought. If you had a 9 percent, thirty-year loan, and you paid about 12.5 percent extra each month, the loan would be paid for in twenty years instead of thirty. In other words, if you had a $700 payment on your house and you paid $788 instead, your house would be paid for ten years early! What would you do if you suddenly found yourself with $788 more disposable income?

The next, more risky investment might be a federally insured bank. As you can tell, we are still way over on the safe end of investments, but the level of risk is not zero. Don't wait until your food supplies and house are paid for before you put money in the bank. That would be ridiculous. Likewise, it doesn't make sense to have tens of thousands of dollars in the bank that could be used for debt reduction, including house payments. It's anybody's guess how much money you should have in the bank, but one suggestion would be to have 30 percent of your yearly income in the bank. I prefer more, because something is bound to come along I didn't figure on. Many investors suggest twelve months' salary of liquid assets that can be withdrawn with only a few days notice. Just as in the game of Monopoly, you can't sell your houses and hotels without paying a penalty. You don't want to use your credit card, so keep at least enough cash in the bank to cover two major disasters in a row.

Diversification is very important for investors, and the same can be true of banks. Suppose that, for some reason, the bank you deal with closes, even for a short time. Suppose the computer forgets who you are for awhile. I recommend you keep your ready cash in at least two banks. That way, if something happens to one bank, you can still use a check from the other bank until they get it straightened out. I suggest that the banks be as dissimilar as possible. Make one a small bank, and the other big. One could be in your hometown and the other in a different state, perhaps near a relative you visit frequently. I also suggest you keep a couple of hundred dollars in small denomination bills in the house. Not too much—you don't want to become a target for crime—but enough to cover a short-term emergency.

At about this level of risk are precious metal coins. Gold and silver coins can be bought from a reputable coin dealer in almost any large town. Gold coins should cost only a little more than the spot price of the bulk metal to purchase. This is not an investment you plan on selling when the price of gold goes up. Think of the coins more as if they were life insurance.

You have probably heard stories of people who salvaged their fortunes during World War II by burying gold coins in bottles in the garden so the Germans couldn't find them. I wouldn't go overboard, but a few gold coins from a recognized mint, stored in a safe place, could turn out to be a valuable asset someday.

Once you have all of the above-mentioned investments well on their way, but not yet carried to completion, you are ready to start to move a little more toward the side of speculation. I suggest you buy into stocks and bonds—mostly stocks—through no-load mutual funds. You don't need a stockbroker, but you need to do some research. One reason I didn't do this earlier in my life, besides my fear that stocks constituted a risky investment, is that I didn't know *how* to do it. I didn't know any stockbrokers, and the thought of going to one intimidated me. As I approached forty, I became concerned that I had put too many of my eggs in one basket. I live in a small, one-employer town in the Mojave Desert, and I worried that if someone decided to close the facility where I worked, the town could blow away and my house with it.

I attended a seminar, paid for by my employer, which explained about the various retirement options available to me. One of my options was a fund that mimicked the Standard and Poor's 500 Index. The S & P 500 is a selection of five hundred stocks designed to represent the stock market. There are several measures of the stock market, such as the

Dow Jones Industrials, but the S & P 500 is as good as any, and better than most. About this time I noticed there was a section in the *U.S. News and World Report,* to which I subscribe, that I was regularly ignoring. This section, contained in certain special issues, compared various mutual funds. Yearly, they list and rate literally hundreds of mutual funds. Several other magazines also present similar material. In fact, some specialize in investments. I decided I should pay more attention, so I started to do my homework. Once I had armed myself with a little information and courage, I experimented by investing in a couple of mutual funds.

A mutual fund is essentially partial ownership in a group of stocks, bonds, or a combination of both. These funds are sold to the public with a small overhead charge for managing the fund, usually around one percent. The "load" is an extra charge, sometimes quite large, which becomes the commission to the stockbroker for selling you the product. Since I suggest you do your own homework, you don't need a broker, or the load charge. Some claim that a loaded fund is better managed and therefore pays a higher yield on your investment. The evidence doesn't bear that out. Therefore, I suggest *no-load mutual funds.* Many of these funds invest in literally a hundred or more different stocks or bonds. Each fund has a different strategy, and a different management team. You need to find a few that meet your needs and your investment objectives.

There are always some hot ones that produce outstanding results for a year or two. May I suggest that you are not interested in a flash in the pan. What I suggest is a long-term performer. Look at the performance record over the last ten years. You're not looking for a fad; instead, you're betting on the overall trend of the market.

A fund referred to as an *aggressive growth fund* invests in relatively risky stocks, often new companies that give the promise of fast profits. When I first started investing I chose one of these, because the fund had done some outstanding things in the recent past. It seemed anything but aggressive after I bought it, so I lost patience and moved my money elsewhere, where I was seeing a more consistent total yield. A *growth fund* is similar to aggressive growth, but not so aggressive, of course. Both growth and aggressive growth funds typically pay few or no dividends. The way you make money is, the stock goes up in value. The difference between the purchase price and the sale price is your profit—or, in other words, the growth.

Funds referred to as *growth-with-income* or *balanced-income funds* are more conservative and fluctuate less than the growth funds. These are more in line with what I would suggest for the bulk of your paper investments. Balanced funds include both stocks and bonds to stabilize the fund and generate a more consistent dividend. *Utility income funds* also are usually a more conservative investment, because utility stocks tend to produce a consistent dividend and show stable growth. All these funds will increase in value over time, but they are geared more toward dividend income rather than growth. On average, the total yield is less than the growth and aggressive growth stocks, but there are fewer peaks and valleys along the way.

There are many other kinds of stock mutual funds, such as those that invest in special industries like leisure or medical. I'm not too wild about these because I am interested in diversifying, not specializing. If any one sector gets hit, you take a big fall. You may choose to put 10 percent or less of your total investment in one or two of these special groups if you have a mind to. (I wouldn't.)

There are various different kinds of bonds. They tend to produce less income than stocks, but the income they do produce is generally more regular, frequently monthly, and they tend to be more stable in price. Long-term corporate and government bonds have averaged around 5 percent over the same sixty-four-year period mentioned before. Just in case you missed the point, let me make it again: Stocks typically do much better than bonds over time, but you must have the guts to stick it out.

There are more kinds of bonds than you can shake a stick at. Municipal bonds have a particular niche, in that most of their income is free of federal taxes. If you are in a high tax bracket, the lower yield can be offset by the tax advantage. Traditionally the advice is to move more from stocks toward bonds as you grow older. This is because you need the income, and because you can no longer afford the time needed to recover from the occasional big drop in the stock market that happens from time to time.

Even though each fund is greatly diversified, with at least twenty different stocks or bonds per fund, I suggest investing in several funds from different families of funds in order to add another level of diversification. Diversifying is very important because it dramatically reduces your risk. If you throw five darts at the investment page of the paper, it is very unlikely you'll hit five losers in a row. I would suggest that five or six different funds would not be too many for the average investor.

In order to invest, all you need to do is pick a fund and call the toll-free number for a prospectus. I wouldn't pick a fund unless it had been rated well and had a proven track record of at least ten years. Once you have done your best to understand the brochures, you mail in your first installment. You can open your account with as little as $1,000 to $3,000. That may sound like a lot of money, but it's not. The interest you pay on car loans, your credit-card balance, and so forth, would probably add up to $3,000 in a couple of years. If it becomes a priority, you will find a way.

Here is where another one of my rules comes into play: You need to have faith in the market and the economy it represents, or you will lose your shirt. Don't take the money out if the market goes down, *no matter what!* When the market is going up, put a little money in your funds; when it is going down, put in even more! The way to make money on the stock market is to do the exact opposite of what your gut tells you.

A friend of mine predicted the stock market for the foreseeable future. It's going to go up, and then it will go down, then it will go up, and then it will go down. He just wasn't sure which it was going to do first. If you buy when it is going up and sell when it goes down, you're making somebody else rich. In 1987, when the market took a dive, a lot of savvy investors bought a lot of stock at very low prices from other investors who got scared. I know of someone who made a fortune off the Great Depression by prudently buying stock at rock-bottom prices from others who sold. If you can't watch your investment fall to half its value and have faith it will eventually recover, you will be clobbered as an investor.

After hundreds of years of experimentation and observation, physicists discovered the four forces that govern the universe. By using the laws described by these forces scientists can explain the universe in rational terms, such as predicting the motions of the planets. If they say that an eclipse will occur on a specific day at a certain time, it will. Before it is detonated, the megatonage of an atomic bomb is also determined using these basic laws. Those four forces are: weak and strong atomic forces, gravity, and electromagnetic attraction. The stock market is governed by only three forces. I will share those three secrets with you so that you can make wiser investments.

The largest force that governs the stock market is the

force of the entire U.S. economy. Companies make things and sell them for a profit. Because of this, they can afford to pay their stockholders dividends, and their stocks grow in value. This is called capitalism; it works very well. Because the economy continues to grow, the stock market as a whole grows at a rate of about 10 percent per year. If you look at a plot of the last hundred years, this upward trend is unmistakable. Of course, there are ups and downs, but these are explained by the other two forces.

The smallest force results in the day-to-day, month-to-month fluctuation of the market. This is where market timers, those who try to buy low and sell high, try to make a killing. Some do. Most don't. The reason this is so is that stock values fluctuate almost randomly over short periods of time. When we're talking days, months, even a couple of years, there is not enough time for the other two forces to prevail. Oh, sure, there are lots of people who have a system. Every one is sure to predict the next Bull or Bear market. There are also people with a lucky arm at the slot machines. Don't you try this. When examined using scientific measures, almost all of these systems work *worse* than tossing a coin.

The reason for this is that people are not predictable over short periods of time. Someone has a bad day and decides to sell. Later he feels lucky and buys. The price of stocks and bonds is a direct result of the whims of millions of investors. Even if you have a huge computer and a large team of analysts, you still can't predict the toss of a penny any better than you can by guessing heads or tails. And the harder you try to beat the system by selling and buying, the more you spend in brokerage fees. The harder you try, the worse it works. There are some subtle trends that can be used as indicators, but you need a lot of money and a fair knowledge of what is happening to take advantage of these trends. Even the best schemes usually don't work much better than just sitting on your investment, however, so I suggest the latter.

There is a special type of fund that takes advantage of this well known but often disbelieved phenomenon. It is called the *index fund*. Over the last two decades they have become much more popular, but they are still very much in the minority among mutual funds. They work like this. The fund buys the same stocks that make up an index, such as the S & P 500, and that is all there is to it. No fancy computer analysis, no high-priced research. It is like getting on a ship without a captain. The funny thing is, they perform better than three-quarters of the competition. Autopilot does work. If you don't have any other money invested, have some money in an index fund of stocks. Once you have a significant sum of money in index funds, you may then want to look into growth funds and others.

The third force fits between the other two forces in terms of time duration. Every time the stock market strays far up or down from the usual 10 percent growth, the market corrects. It may take years to do so, but as long as the economy continues to function, the market continues to follow its faithful climb. For short periods of time, as in the late 1920s or before the crash of 1987, the market will grow much faster than 10 percent per year. Sooner or later, fast or slow, the market corrects. But the problem is, like earthquakes and hurricanes, no one can predict when the correction will occur, only that it eventually will. And while you're waiting for the big correction, chances are you're missing the long-term growth of the market. If you don't believe me, read some of the books I list later that have been written by some of the market experts. They will tell you the same thing.

Don't go for the killing. Don't try to get rich in a year. Try to ride the wave at the same speed as everybody else. The way to invest is to buy shares in several mutual funds, judiciously chosen, and hold them for a long time. It sounds stupid, but it is just that simple. If you constantly churn your investments, buying and selling, pursuing the holy grail of stocks, someone will get rich, but it won't be you.

What you should be betting on is the basic trend of the market. Buy some, then buy some more. Many advisors suggest a scheme called time-cost averaging. The idea is simply to invest the same dollar amount every month. On average this is a good idea. If you do this, you will move along with the general trend of about 10 percent per year, taking your ups and downs. You can do this automatic investing from your checking account each month.

Remember, you never take the money out until you reach the predetermined event you were saving for, such as retirement. My plan is to start collecting the dividends when I retire, instead of reinvesting them as I currently do. I intend to leave the principal to my children when both my wife and I are gone. That way, it doesn't matter how long I live—the principal investment will not diminish. I will still keep receiving dividends, as long as high inflation or a stock market crash doesn't wipe me out. If inflation does clobber my paper investments, that's what my house, food storage, and a few gold coins are for.

Many don't want to get into the stock market for fear that it will collapse and never recover. They fear if that happens they will lose all their money, so they don't invest. Which reminds me of a joke I heard about a couple of terrorists on their way to blow up a building. The terrorist on the passenger side of the car looked in the back seat as he got in and noticed a bomb sitting there, set to explode. He exclaimed, "What are you doing! What if the bomb goes off while we are on our way to the target!" "Don't worry," the driver replied, "I've got another bomb in the trunk."

If the stock market crashes and never recovers, we have

a lot more to worry about than the money we lost in the crash. If K-Mart goes broke, life goes on. Other stores will take its place. Even if GM sputters to a stop, the economy will heal and move on. But if most of corporate America goes out of business at the same time, *then* we're talking catastrophe! Everyone will lose their jobs. Pensions will collapse. The government will be unable to govern. If Wall Street goes down and doesn't recover—well, you can run, but you can't hide.

Earth could be hit by a comet, too, but I wouldn't worry about it. I'm not trying to say that either can't happen; it's just that there is nothing rational I can do to protect myself against the financial equivalent of an all-out nuclear war. The only thing I can imagine that would adequately protect you from a total financial collapse is to sell everything you have *now,* and move to a South Pacific island, and never look back. If you consider that a bit extreme, then join the club. In the meantime, you might as well get out of bed in the morning and live another day. Yes, you may get hit by a truck on the way to work, but that's just a risk you'll have to take. And while you do, go ahead and invest. There is one sure thing: If the market does go up, you only get any dividends on the money you invest.

Don't think you now know enough to start investing just because you read this chapter. This is just a place to start. Do your homework before you send in your check. Read some magazines on the subject, so you know the difference be-tween a dividend and a capital gain, for example. Let me suggest a few books I found interesting:

Everyone's Money Book, by Jordan E. Goodman and Sonny Bloch. With over eight hundred pages this book looks very intimidating, but it is a must-read. You need to know the basics, and this book has the basics on a lot of financial subjects. You don't need to read the whole book cover to cover—I didn't—but you need to read enough to be familiar with the terms. Think of it as an encyclopedia. Their approach is very much like an encyclopedia, with the material laid out in a logical easy-to-read format. My one major complaint about the book is the authors' treatment of the personal budget. Their approach reminds me of a 1040 form without the instructions, only more complicated. Of course, I like my approach much better. Other than that, I think this is a great place to start learning about investments.

A Random Walk Down Wall Street, by Burton G. Malkiel. This is another must-read. Mr. Malkiel leads you through several philosophies about the stock market, both good and bad, in a readable, fascinating book. A lot of my investment philosophy comes from this book and others like it. The book is about a hundred pages too long, because Malkiel never just makes a point—he pounds it into the ground. Nevertheless, you need to read this book. I won't steal his thunder; *read the book.* Don't miss the listing of recommended mutual funds in the back.

Contrarian Investment Strategy (The Psychology of Stock-Market Success), by David Dreman. If your local library doesn't have *A Random Walk Down Wall Street,* read *Contrarian Investment Strategy.* This is also a great book; there is, however, a lot of overlap between the two. They even tell some of the same stories. The difference is, this book proposes that you can make a little more than the average by moving in the opposite direction of the crowd. There are mutual funds that subscribe to that philosophy, and historically they have done better than most.

Beating the Street, by Peter Lynch. In Peter Lynch's opinion, you should do your own investing rather than going to a mutual fund. You could say that I am including his book to give equal time for opposing views. For thirteen years he ran what became one of the largest and most successful mutual funds in America, the Fidelity Magellan Fund. During that time, a $1,000 investment in Magellan Fund increased to $28,000! I guess he has earned the right to have a differing point of view. However, there are two things he glosses over: One is that you need at least $100,000 to get started buying stocks in large enough quantities for a diverse portfolio; the other is that he does things like hobnob with CEOs of the world's largest companies. They may return *his* calls, but somehow I doubt they would return calls from good-old-what's-his-name, Steve Johnson. As long as there are successful fund managers like Peter Lynch, why not jump on the bandwagon?

I must add that I took great interest in the fact that at the time he wrote his book, after all the success he'd achieved, Lynch was still driving a fifteen-year-old AMC Concord. Not exactly the trendy thing to do. I think this proves two things: First, Peter Lynch has much better things to do with his money than waste it on fancy new cars every three years—like invest it, for example. The second is, when you're really successful, you don't need to put on a show to prove anything to your neighbors.

Remember, you don't have to be an expert, you just need to know what you're doing. Think of it this way—you don't need to pick the winner, you just need to pick the average.

Suppose you were betting on a horse race. There are, let's say, twenty horses in the race. If you pick the fastest horse you win big. If you pick one of the other nineteen horses you get nothing. Not much of a sure thing, is it?

Now let's start the race over. This time you get to bet on as many horses as you like. If most of the horses you pick do average, you get about a 10 percent increase on your bet. Sounds a lot easier, doesn't it? You don't even care if you bet on the winning horse or not. Eventually, if you just stick with it, you can do very well. Do you think that, if you bet on six horses for twenty consecutive races, you could pick some average horses? If you buy an index fund you know it will come in fifth in a field of twenty, every time. This is better than having an uncle whose friend's brother knows a jockey! But you must be disciplined. If you keep pursuing the killing, you could pick a loser every race. Spread your investment around, and don't keep changing your mind. You need to be patient.

Moving along, land can be another good investment, *if* you want to put up with the hassle. This is especially true of a rental. My wife and I did that for a while, but the problems of being a landlord were more than we wanted to put up with. Also remember that real estate can be risky, too, often more risky than the stock market. The positive side of real estate is that land is tangible. The problem is, if things go sour, you could be making a payment on an asset that generates no income. Investing in stocks and bonds can be interrupted, if necessary, at any time. If you quit making payments on your real estate investment, the bank will take it back and you lose everything. Another advantage of stocks and bonds is that you aren't tied to any particular part of the country, as you are with land. Sometimes local economies can be devastated while the country as a whole does fine. Still, land is something that is not an abstraction.

There are other investments, such as junk bonds, commodities, and roulette wheels. Personally, I don't recommend them. I believe most reputable financial counselors would agree with me on that.

Let me say just a word about taxes. On second thought, never mind. I don't believe there is one single soul in the entire world who understands the U.S. tax code. Not only that, the tax code changes year to year, sometimes radically. With a little luck, Congress will come to their senses soon and scrap the whole income-tax system, and start over. In the meantime, investments will make your taxes a little more complicated, but not that much worse. Every year there are several books published that specialize in taxes. If you have a question buy one of these, or, if you're really ambitious, send off for one of the free publications the government provides. Taxes take a bit out of your profits, but for now they still take no more than 32 percent. That's better than leaving you with nothing.

There is one thing about taxes that is very important. Whenever you sell stocks, bonds, land, or almost any other investment, you need to pay capital gains on the difference between the sale price and the purchase price. As long as you don't sell, you don't have to pay. That alone is a good argument for not buying and selling your investments frequently. When you die your estate is revalued, so your beneficiaries start with a clean slate. This is one scheme to beat the tax man, but unfortunately, the someone who has to die to take advantage of this scheme is you.

As I write this book I am already, in my forties, beginning to reap the benefits from sacrifices my wife and I made long ago. A common sacrifice that many people make, myself included, is a college education. There was no guarantee of a more lucrative existence stapled to the back of my diploma, but, along with millions of others, I found doors open to me that wouldn't have been otherwise. This happened because I was willing to stick out some tough times for a few years.

The most likely scenario, in my opinion, is that my company retirement will not be sufficient to retire on, and neither will my investments. I hope that both will be sufficient to get me by. History is on my side. It's not likely that the United States will cease to exist, nor is it likely that everything will be just peachy. The alternative to investing is to spend it all now, in which case you can be certain that you will be at someone else's mercy when you get old. Currently half of Americans claim they can't afford to retire at age sixty-five. My plan is to be among the other half—how about you? Investing 5 or 10 percent of your income could make all the difference in the world.

Have you ever noticed that most surfers ride the front of the wave, rather than the back? Why do you suppose that is? It takes more effort to get in front of the wave, but, once you do, it makes the ride much easier. Just imagine that wave curling up behind you as you slide ever forward. Let your money push you, rather than constantly trying to catch up. There are no guarantees to any of the suggestions I have just listed; but, if you don't try, you can't win.

Chapter 13
What God Hath Joined Together

About half way through one of the six-week seminars I taught, I asked the audience how they were doing. One of the wives responded that she and her husband had had the biggest fight of their marriage as a result of talking about their budget. She stated it in a kind of joking manner, and I doubt that anyone in the audience considered for one second that their marriage was in any serious danger. However, there was enough emphasis in her voice that I, at least, accepted at face value that they'd had a real humdinger of a discussion about money.

One of the benefits I am certain will come from carefully managing your money is that it will decrease the strain, and therefore increase the pleasure, of living together as a family. The wife's statement seems to fly in the face of that argument. What I believe actually happened was that a fight, which was inevitable given their lack of financial planning to that point, had been moved forward in time. Without planning for retirement they would have had a rude awakening someday, and it would probably would have been much worse. What taking the class did was give then more time to do something about their finances, before they found themselves in a bad situation with no time left to fix it.

However, if the cure kills the patient, it isn't much of a cure. It is very important that relationships between spouses be treated very carefully. Calling each other names and laying blame is anything but constructive. I am no family counselor, and I feel a bit out of my field talking about this subject, but the subject is so important, and so critical to the success of the budget, that I will take a stab at it, anyway.

Let me first start by dispelling the myth that women don't manage money as well as men. It is often convenient to believe this, if you're a man, but to this point, I haven't found a shred of evidence to support such an argument. I haven't kept track of statistics, but so far, I have found there are just as many irresponsible males as females, and I have found more than one woman whose tightfistedness I have found absolutely inspiring.

What I have consistently found is that most adults are, to some degree, receptive to improving their finances, but usually they aren't aware of how to go about it, or simply aren't motivated enough to do what they already know. A significant portion of those I've taught beam with feelings of self-worth once they've taken control of their finances. On the other hand, some others seem trapped in a self-destructive rut and determined to stay on that course at all costs.

On occasion I have counseled people individually. When I do this, I try never to let the participants place blame on each other for past behavior. I avoid this pitfall by talking about the couple fixing their finances as if the two spouses are mutually under attack by an enemy. The fact is, they really are. The only question is whether they will unite and succeed, or divide and self-destruct. I believe it is far more effective to depersonalize the problem, rather than to imply that one or both partners are guilty of some sin. Even if they want to improve their finances, most people, if verbally attacked, recoil into a defensive position from which little can be accomplished.

The only way you will ever solve your financial problems is by working together. One of the characteristics of a healthy family relationship is that both of the spouses have covenanted to work together for the common good. I have noticed that the couples who are intent on placing blame on each other are the ones that I can do the least to help. If you do work together, there is a synergistic effect you can take advantage of. Together, the strengths of both adults build a force that is stronger than the sum added separately.

I am usually in a hurry when I want something, so if I find what I am looking for, I buy it, but I carefully watch the bottom line. This means I often pass up buying something to keep the budget in balance. My wife, Laurel, typically takes a lot of time shopping for something, and by the time she's finally bought it, she usually has the best deal in town. Historically, however, she hasn't worried as much about the bottom line, only that each individual purchase was a good deal. Since we have been married we have blended our buying habits, which is better than either approach alone.

Whenever I talk about finances, someone always asks, "What does your wife think about it? Doesn't she feel controlled?" The truth is, she appreciates it. She also knows that she is not the only person who is being controlled by the budget. Whenever we talk about each other's strengths, she always includes the fact that I am a good provider and a good manager of money. I always include the fact that she is careful with the money I worked so hard to earn. If you know Laurel, you know that she has many truly outstanding traits. Being careful with our money is one of them. It is true that, on occasion, she chides me for being too tight with money, and occasionally I get after her for spending money a little too freely. The truth is, we are probably both correct to a certain degree.

One of the worst mistakes some spouses make while working on their finances is that they don't communicate;

instead, they shout. Most people think, for some reason, that if they can just yell loud enough the other person will suddenly see their point of view. Obviously they assume they have married a deaf person. If you find that the volume is getting a bit high—in other words, the neighbors are coming out to see who's winning—take a break. Nothing constructive will come of continuing the "discussion."

Try this instead: Take turns talking. In fact, do more than that. After your spouse has spoken, uninterrupted, repeat back to your spouse what you think he or she just said. Notice in the fictitious conversations I included in chapters 5, 6, and 7 that is exactly what my character the financial counselor did. Also notice that, in chapter 7, my character realized he was mistaken about the assumptions he had made. Don't assume you know what your spouse is saying until you have repeated it back to him or her, and he or she has agreed that you do, in fact, understand.

Never do what I did in chapter 5. Never make fun of or belittle your spouse about his or her ability to manage money, or anything else. It may be humorous in a book, but it is definitely not helpful in real life. If you have ever offended your spouse, stop reading this book right now and go apologize, no matter how long ago it happened. I've had to apologize several times to my wife. If you do belittle your spouse, all you have done is plant a land mine in your marriage; sooner or later, you will step on it. I suggest you get rid of it now. Also, never go telling other people about your spouse's weaknesses, unless you are in a genuine quest for truth and are asking in strictest confidence for help in solving your problems. Whenever I have counseled with people and they start to blame each other, I try to get them to quit. You will never get anywhere unless you work together.

Start by talking together about what goals you both

have. "Just think; if we pay off the home loan early, we could buy a cabin in the mountains with the money we save."

"You know, if we don't start saving for college now, we will never be able to send the kids to college. Don't you agree?"

"Darling, we have to start saving for a better car. That old clunker is even worse than the last one we had."

"Darling, I'll bet you're about as fed up with these bills as I am. Those credit-card companies are getting all the money we could be spending on something for us! What do you say we start a budget and see if we can't get out from under some of these bills."

"You know, dear, we need to start saving for a new house. This neighborhood is going to the dogs. I'll bet you don't feel safe around here anymore, do you?"

"I don't believe we will get more than a quarter of what we put into Social Security when we get old. Let's start investing so we don't have to eat doggie bits."

Don't assume you know how to do things better than your spouse. Chances are, you both have some great ideas that will be the best solution for your particular situation. Try to see it his or her way. Try reversing roles for a while. One reason my wife is so appreciative of me is that she worked as a librarian and then as a teacher before we got married; she knows it isn't easy to make money. I also do the shopping frequently. It's important that you see the other side of the fence sometimes.

One of the things you are going to have to do is compromise. You will never find a solution where both parties get everything they want. Be willing to give up something you want for something else you want even more.

Both my living daughters, Mindy and Michelle, are adopted. Mindy was 4½ months old when we adopted her, but Michelle came home with us the day after she was born.

Laurel wanted very much to nurse Michelle, even though Laurel had not been pregnant lately. She made the appropriate contacts with the La Leche League and the Lactation Institute in Encino, and then presented the plan to me. I agreed, but neither of us realized how difficult it would turn out to be. Laurel had to pump every two hours almost twenty-four hours a day to stimulate her lactation to prepare for nursing. When we got the baby, Laurel would feed her with a periodontal syringe filled with what Laurel had pumped, supplemented with formula, while the baby sucked.

The baby's sucking at the breast stimulated the milk supply, as formula mixed with mother's milk supplemented the diet. Slowly, bit by bit, the milk supply increased as we labored day after day and week after week. I would stay up late at night to clean the equipment, help with the feedings, and do other things that needed to be done. This went on for months, but the supply just wasn't catching up like it should. Michelle would suck so softly Laurel just wasn't getting the stimulation our coach at the Institute expected, based on previous experience.

Finally, we got a call from the Institute. The coach had suddenly noticed, from a picture she had taken of the baby while her mouth was open, that Michelle was more tongue-tied than the coach had previously thought. She, the doctor, and a dentist had all seen the symptoms of being tongue-tied, but each had concluded they weren't significant enough to make a difference to the nursing. We had Michelle's tongue clipped free so that she could nurse better, and suddenly she was able to give up the little bit of formula she was still receiving.

I tell you this story for a couple of reasons. The only way that Laurel would have been able to nurse the baby is if I had done everything I could to make it possible. I'm not a great cook and housekeeper, but I did as much as I could. I went with her to all her visits every two weeks in Encino, more than one hundred miles away. It was Laurel's turn to get all the support the family could muster.

I couldn't have written this book without her help. Just the moral support alone is very important. Sometimes I take a break from writing to go do the dishes, but right now it's my turn to get the lion's share of the family effort. Family finances are the same way. You have to compromise for the good of the whole family. There just isn't enough to do everything all at once.

Another reason I related the story is that we can use the analogy of Michelle's eating to our own financial diet. Most people don't need to work harder; they need to work smarter. If you're not being efficient with your money, you will find yourself working until you are exhausted without reaching your goal. Michelle was sucking as hard as she could, but there were forces holding her back that needed to be removed. Using a budget is like setting yourself free to be more efficient. To be more efficient, you need to work together.

Everybody has some little area where they want to have their way. It is a way of reducing stress and giving you the feeling that you have some control over your own destiny. One of the things I like is to listen to music while I am working. Out of my category I have bought portable stereos (boom boxes) for almost every room in the house, and for the garage. Laurel doesn't particularly like to listen to the radio, but she encourages me: "If that's what you want, go ahead and buy it. You earned it." Of course, she also has her favorite things she likes to buy. That is why it is so important that each spouse have his own category, which he or she has complete control over.

Each person has some area they are not willing to negotiate over. I am reminded of a true story I was told about a couple who were applying for a divorce. At that time, the laws of California required that a reason must be stated for the divorce. When the lawyer asked for the reason the couple were applying for a divorce, the wife responded that her husband spit in the sink. The lawyer was a little taken aback by this. He asked the husband if it was so; the husband confirmed the allegation, and furthermore volunteered that he was not about to stop, either.

Apparently the husband's mother had taught him that, when you chew tobacco, you don't spit on the floor but in the sink. The wife, on the other hand, fixed dinner in the sink, and she was not about to let anybody spit in her clean sink.

The lawyer knew this would never work in front of a judge, so he continued to ask questions of the wife, fishing for something that would stand up in court as grounds for divorce.

"Does your husband ever drink?"

"Sure."

"Does he drink to excess?"

"Usually."

"When he is drunk, does he ever beat you?"

"Sure, all the time."

"Well, don't you think that is grounds for divorce?"

"Oh no! He doesn't know what he's doing. He's drunk. He can't help it. But when he *spits* in my clean sink, he's *stone sober!*"

The lawyer went to court, asked the right questions, which he carefully worded, and never once mentioned spitting in her clean sink. The divorce was granted.

The reason their marriage ended in divorce is not that they had areas that were nonnegotiable. It ended in divorce because the nonnegotiable areas overlapped, which resulted in an insoluble confrontation. As long as both parties are willing to give a little, a workable solution is reachable. If both parties stake out a section of the income and there isn't enough left over to run the family, then disaster is inevitable.

Try this. Start by laying out the items of your budget that are fixed—in other words, things you can't change. Your house payment is probably fixed. You can't cut it, unless you want to be evicted. Come to an agreement on what you are saving for. Put this up front so that future needs will not be sacrificed to immediate wants. List things that you have some control over, like utilities, and allot an amount close to, but less than, what you have been spending for them in the past. This is how you will get more for other things like savings. It may mean you will have to be more careful about the food you buy, or lower the thermostat in the winter, but something has to give. Once these are covered, the rest is left to divide between the spouses; these are the very important discretionary funds. If everything doesn't add up, try it again.

Usually what happens is that a long list of necessities comes out and there just isn't enough money to go around. Let me suggest a concept to you. Generally, most parents consider braces for their children a necessity. My wife had a playground accident when she was in the first grade that resulted in her nose being broken. Although significant damage was done, it wasn't apparent at first, and her mouth formed incorrectly as a result. Later a very painful operation was performed, which improved her breathing, but her teeth were still not straight.

When she was in college she went to an orthodontist and asked what would have to be done to straighten her teeth. He told her that there wasn't enough bone to move her teeth through, so her top front six teeth would have to be removed, her bone reconstructed, and her teeth replaced. There was a risk she would lose the teeth and a bridge would have to be substituted if the replaced teeth died. She thanked the doctor politely, and left his office determined to leave her teeth right where they were. She has survived for more than two decades since then, even though her teeth are not straight. The pain and suffering were not worth any benefit that would result from fixing her teeth.

May I suggest that the financial pain and suffering that will result from spending money you don't have are every bit as real as the pain Laurel would have endured in order to have her teeth fixed. If your kids need braces and you have decided it is a necessity, be prepared to cut something else!

Some people are simply belligerent and will not compromise; they fight any effort to make a budget work. They will not allow any budget to interfere with the things they feel entitled to buy. Often two people of this type find each other and marry. I personally find this situation extremely depressing and disturbing. As far as I am concerned, the marriage has already terminated. Even if the two people manage to stay together, and some manage to do so for years, the fighting and anger is nothing I would care to endure. There is no hope until someone starts being more cooperative.

Although my reaction to a belligerent spouse would probably be to give up in disgust and walk out the door, I don't suggest it. Sometimes people change. It may take years, but so do child support and alimony payments. If you are in this situation, don't give up. Try just getting rid of the credit cards, limit the use of the checkbook to paying utilities, and try living off cash for everything else. Do whatever is reasonable to make a deal. However, as with drugs or alcohol, some people have to crash and burn before they can start to work their way back to sanity.

Usually people are this way because they think they deserve it. It may be the example they observed in their parents as they grew up, or it may be a way of compensating for feelings of inadequacy. Whatever it is, a frontal assault is rarely the answer. Try negotiating by exchanging something else they want for better control over the finances. If they simply dig in their heels and won't budge or compromise over an extended period of time, then, whether you like it or not, your marriage is doomed. It may be sooner, or it may be later, but the depressing end result is that you will almost certainly separate.

While you're doing this evaluating, consider yourself. Are you the belligerent one? Are you compromising? Is this really just a way to exert your own power and dominion? Before you start straightening out your spouse, be sure you are straight first.

Marriage is a magic thing. If you work together consistently and systematically, you can prepare for whatever is coming down the road. And what is coming down the road may not be pretty.

Chapter 14
A Look in the Dark Crystal

When you get through with this chapter you may feel so depressed that you would like to put this book down and never open it again. I must urge you to read on. After you have read this chapter take a break, if you feel you must, but you need to read chapter 15 as well. I don't just rain doom and gloom; there are solutions. However, if I don't spell out the difficulties we face, the solutions may seem too extreme. So grit your teeth and read on.

Why do I talk like the ship is sinking and there isn't much time to get in the lifeboats? Do I know something nobody else knows? Do I know that the American economy is about to collapse? First, let's get one thing straight; I'm not an economist, I'm an engineer. Furthermore, I'm not privy to any information on the subject that isn't available to the general public. However, I know this much—if I were a frog, and the water kept getting hotter, I would get out of the pot, not go for a swim.

I'm not about to make any hard and fast predictions about the future, complete with the dates I expect doomsday to arrive. I don't believe anybody can calculate the specific economic future with any certainty, any more then we can predict in detail some other person's destiny. Among other things, the future is dependent on future decisions that have yet to be made. But if you saw a boy, constantly into mischief, you wouldn't have to be a prophet to say, "If that boy doesn't straighten up, sooner or later, he's going to find himself in a lot of trouble." Well, I think that we are that boy.

There have been authors who saw reckless public financial policies and made predictions of utter disaster, sometimes with specific dates that have come and gone. The problem with crying wolf too many times is that you lose credibility, which is necessary when the wolf finally shows up. Imminent earthquakes on the San Andreas fault have been predicted most of my life. The fact that the San Andreas fault is about thirty years overdue for a massive earthquake shouldn't make anyone complacent.

More than once I have been dismissed as an eternal pessimist. In fact, they claim, I wouldn't know good news if it came up and bit me. They may be right. I wonder, sometimes, if I haven't painted things too dark by searching too hard for things that could go wrong. But engineers don't look for things that are working, only things that are broken or about to break. If we had a car, and we were about to go across the desert in the summer, I would look under the hood before we leave. If I found a good carburetor, good spark plugs, and a radiator hose that was about to burst, I wouldn't say, "Well, two out of three ain't bad." Let me list some of the things I lose sleep over, and you decide if I'm overreacting.

I think there are three factions in America who, for their own personal gain, have shown very poor financial judgment over the last several decades, putting all of us in serious peril. Those three groups are the federal government, corporate America, and the average American citizen. Did I miss anybody? What each of them did is go unbelievably far into debt.

Let's start with the federal government. I could tell you that it is 4.5 gazillion dollars in debt, but I doubt it would mean any more to you than it does to me. Million, billion, trillion, I deal with very large and very small numbers at work every day, yet still all those "illions" remain incomprehensible. But I'll tell you what I *can* understand. I understand $56,000. That's how much my share of the federal debt was in 1991, according to the 1993 *World Almanac*. That is based on the assumption that I am the head of an average family of four. As I write this book, in 1995, I know that the number is now closer to $75,000. In 1980, it was about $16,000. Since about 1980, the national debt has been doubling every six years. That is equivalent to an increase of about 12 percent per year. The previous couple of decades it grew at about 9 percent per year.

I can tell you that it is impossible for deficit spending to continue at that rate for very much longer. It is impossible for it to continue at even half that rate. How can I say that? It's simple. The Federal Reserve keeps the economy growing at about 2½ to 3 percent per year to keep inflation in check. How can we increase the debt at 12 or even 6 percent per year, if the economy increases at only 3 percent?!

You don't have to understand what a trillion is in order to understand that if you are in a hole and dirt is falling in faster than you can throw the dirt back out, you are going to be buried alive! If the government continues to spend more than it collects at an ever-increasing rate, eventually the debt would consume the entire value of everything in the country. Soon after that it would consume the net value of the entire world. That is impossible! It cannot happen. Something will change, and change is often painful.

While you are trying to digest that, let me give you some more good news. The government does something that is very interesting. It keeps a second set of books. The second set of books includes what it officially refers to as "off-budget expenses." Remember the savings and loan bailout? That,

115

and many other expenses, end up "off budget." I have heard estimates that put off-budget expenses almost as high as on-budget expenses. If that is true, then we are even closer to being buried alive than the official numbers would indicate.

I said it can't continue. What will keep it from continuing? One possibility is that the government will continue to borrow ever greater amounts of money until they exhaust the entire world's credit limit. I have no idea how far off that date is, but it is not decades. I suspect that, should we follow that course, institutions will do their best to keep everything running as smoothly as possible right up to the last minute. One day we will be doing fine; the next, everything will collapse. Then all hell will break loose!

What happens when the welfare office shuts down and recipients are told to "come back next month, we may have some information for you then"? Over 10 percent of Americans are dependent on welfare from the government. That doesn't include Social Security, salaried federal employees, and many others who receive their living directly or indirectly from the government. About half of the residents of the state of California in one way or another receive their income from government, and the percentage is still growing. What happens when Social Security benefits get cut by one-third, or discontinued all together? What happens when millions of Americans get turned out of their jobs and unemployment insurance is cut to only two weeks?

Maybe everybody will roll up their sleeves and start over, rebuilding from scratch. (If they do, then I guess I have been a gloomy pessimist. Yet somehow I can't imagine that happening.)

There is another possibility. Do you remember the riots in Los Angeles after the verdict of the Rodney King trial? The verdict was read a few days before the end of the month.

After about three days of rioting, it was announced that the mail would not be delivered due to the riots. Therefore, to receive welfare checks people had to go to the post office to collect their checks in person. The riots ended suddenly and huge lines appeared at the post office. Did the riot end because of the welfare checks, or because of the presence of the National Guard, or because people just got tired of the rioting? I suspect it was all of the above and more, but I can't help but wonder what will happen everywhere when the checks just suddenly stop coming.

Before I go on, let me make one thing extremely clear: I am not a racist! But racism is alive and well in America. What's more, racism is not limited to any one race.

In 1965 when federal agencies were dragging the rivers of Mississippi looking for the bodies of three missing social workers, they found the bodies of nine black men they hadn't even been looking for. White Aryan Race, Skinheads, KKK; they follow different banners, but their aims are all too familiar and their ranks are swelling. Conversely look at the LA riots, where black-owned shops advertised their status, knowing full well whom the preferred targets of the rioters were. Fear among many whites of violence at the hands of black youths is not just a figment of their imagination. Don't forget the Hispanic, Vietnamese, or Korean gang members who hate and, in turn, are hated. The list goes on and on.

So, what happens when some of the welfare recipients, black, white, or brown, who had no business being on the dole in the first place, find that the government isn't giving out money anymore? Far too many know only how to collect welfare from their "old lady" and hang around. Many don't care if they go to prison, because their quality of life is about the same inside or out. Either way, life stinks and the government provides.

What happens when millions of Americans, who used

117

to have a job, suddenly find themselves out of work and out of money? What happens when someone tells that newly unemployed worker that some other ethnic group destroyed the job? Without the job, the newly unemployed worker has all the time in the world to think about it.

"They did it to the black man again! They have pushed you down with slavery for four hundred years, and now they are going to starve you! It's time we got even with the white man once and for all!"

"It's the fault of those blacks down in the ghetto making babies and collecting welfare checks! They ruined America!"

"It's the illegal immigrants that did it! They come across the border to take our jobs and live off the welfare system. Send them back where they belong!"

"It's those gooks that did it! We should have left them in 'Nam where they belong!"

"It's all the fault of the Jews. Those Jewish bankers are getting rich while the country starves! They ruined Germany! Kill the Jews! *Sieg Heil! Sieg Heil! Sieg Heil!*"

You think it can't happen in America? I agree, it can't, as long as most people are fed and housed, as long as the government keeps paying to make it so. It couldn't happen in Germany without massive unemployment and hyper-inflation. Both communist and fascist groups experienced massive increases in membership in America in the 1930s, when there were more Americans out of work and hungry than at any other time.

Do I think that the United States government will be overthrown by fascists? No, I do not. Nor do I think it will be overthrown by any other radical dictatorial group. But that doesn't mean it won't be bloody trying to keep the civil unrest from burning American cities to the ground. I believe that anyone under the age of sixty will very likely see, during their lifetime, the bloodiest civil strife in America since the

Civil War. I believe the only reason the attempt to take over America will fail is that too many Americans will simply refuse to fall for half lies and hate mongering. But unfortunately hundreds of thousands, maybe millions, will.

Don't I feel for the poor in America? You bet I do! I've been poor. I've been hungry. There are people that I care about who are, or have been, on welfare. And yes, I know that not everyone who accepts welfare is a doper or a thief. I also know that Social Security, Medicare, and other programs are at least as responsible for busting the budget as welfare, but, especially in times of crises, it is easier to shovel the blame on someone else rather than to accept shared blame. In fact, we got exactly the government we wanted and voted for, and most of us bellied up to the trough while the debt grew year after year. But the party is almost over. The situation is coming to a climax, and it must change radically or disaster will result.

How about corporate America? Maybe big business can bail out the government with higher corporate taxes. The corporate debt ratio went up drastically, from about 50 percent to about 75 percent during the 1980s. I don't know what it is now, but I wouldn't bet on killing that goose while it is laying golden eggs. If you strip corporations of their profits, they have no choice but to lay off more workers to stay in business and keep paying their investors. Remember the investors. Corporations are owned by people. That's you! How long would you leave your money invested if you received little or no return on it while the risk remained high? If you wouldn't do it, don't expect anybody else to do it, either.

How about the average American—you know, the hard working, thrifty American? Well, the last I heard, about four years ago, he was about $20,000 in debt, not including his home loan! I couldn't believe that number until I realized that one car bought on time could easily be $15,000 to $30,000. Add a car that is half paid for to a couple of credit cards, and there you are. You don't even need a student loan or medical bills. The average American has not prepared for financial difficulty.

So, let's figure this out. Suppose some average family still owes $60,000 on their typical $100,000 home. Suppose they owe the average $20,000 on other personal debt. Then quadruple their share of the national debt from $75,000 to $300,000 over the next twelve or maybe sixteen years. Do you think we can keep up with higher government spending by raising taxes? Good luck!

There are other possible scenarios. In the 1960s the economy grew so fast that the national debt, which had mushroomed during World War II, dwindled in comparison to the size of the economy. The ratio of national debt to GNP fell from .55 to .36 during the '60s. (See the graph on the following page.) However, I wouldn't expect a repeat of that any time soon. Our industrial base was unique after the destruction of the war, and the international competition is a lot stronger today. In the 1970s inflation grew so fast that the debt-to-GNP ratio shrunk still further, to .33. In other words, because of inflation, the value of the money we'd borrowed eroded, which made the debt ratio less. However, this was achieved at the expense of raising the cost of everything we buy. Most of those who remember double-digit inflation don't want that again. In response to high inflation, the Federal Reserve reined in the money supply in order to restore a reasonable rate of inflation at the end of the '70s and the beginning of the '80s, thereby precipitating a deep recession. During the 1980s without inflation to hide behind, the debt-to-GNP ratio grew from .33 to .58. That last jump in the ratio ought to sober anyone.

The government could make a pre-emptive strike by

decreasing the rate of growth of government spending, at least to a level that could be sustained. To be fair to the federal government, the deficit has been significantly reduced, starting with the last year of the Bush administration and continuing into the first few years under Clinton. Most of that resulted from a cyclical economy, and from defense cuts. But we still haven't cut nearly enough, nor is the deficit projected to stay as low as it is currently without some drastic reductions. Even if we cut the deficit to nothing, a financial burden is still there because of the total debt we've accumulated over the years. Remember, the *deficit* is how much we add to the debt in a given year. Total *debt* is how much we have borrowed so far. Because of a lack of caring on the part of the voters, and a lack of unified will on the part of politicians, I

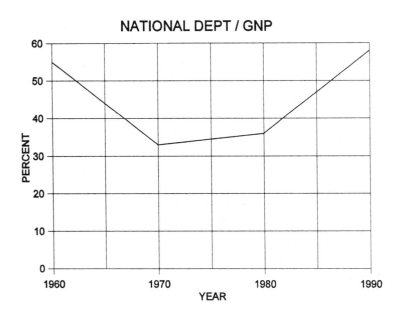

NATIONAL DEPT / GNP

personally doubt that any real solution will appear until it is too late, but you never know.

If the Congress carries through with its current plan to balance the budget and cuts spending a lot more than it has so far, I believe the economy will stagger along awhile until it eventually recovers. If history repeats itself and legislators fail to fix the problem, the day of reckoning will come. They may cut it just enough to keep the creditors at bay. Rather than ending in a fiery crash, we may die the death of a thousand cuts.

So far, the only portion of the budget to have been cut appreciably is defense. The military has been cut so much, and enough new flash points have surfaced to which we have sent troops, that currently there are not enough active army divisions of sufficient strength to execute another Desert Storm without crippling our other commitments. Some other parts of the military are similarly affected, but not to the same degree. The entitlements, which collectively are much bigger than defense, must be cut whether we like it or not. Maybe, by the time this book is in print, Social Security, Medicare, and the rest will all be on a diet. Until they are, we can't cut enough. On our current course, entitlements will eventually consume the entire national budget!

This is, of course, the point at which I'm supposed to lay all the blame on Washington. Let me make one, often over-looked, observation: The United States is not a monarchy; neither is it a dictatorship. We elected every one of those senators and representatives, along with the president. The reason they can't make significant cuts in the deficit, let alone in the national debt, is that if they did, they wouldn't make it from the Capitol Building to their car for the mobs of irate citizens. No, we can blame them all we want, and call for term limits and the like, but the truth is, *we*, the American people, are addicted to the goodies coming from Washington, and there is no way to get off an addiction without pain!

Whether we balance the budget or not, collectively we are all going to have to pay more just to maintain the standard we have become used to. We cannot forever keep borrowing from the future the way we have; the future is here—now.

Let's change the subject. I went to my insurance agent the other day to add earthquake insurance to my home owner's policy. I had resisted buying it because I figured, living ninety miles from the San Andreas fault, that when the big one came, the damage done to my home would be little more than the deductible, so I would collect little or nothing. I also figured that there would be so much damage done to the Los Angeles Valley that the insurance companies would go broke long before I got a dime. As a result of the Landers earthquake, which was not on the San Andreas but out in the desert, I decided that the risk of a local earthquake was too great to ignore, so I bought earthquake insurance, just in case.

While I was there my agent told me a few things about the Northridge quake, which had just occurred. The Northridge quake resulted in claims against the company of over ten times what was expected for an earthquake of that magnitude. The total cost of the Northridge earthquake was about $20 billion. The Oakland fires and Loma Preienta earthquake cost about $5 billion each. The Mississippi flood of 1993 cost about $12 billion. Hurricane Andrew caused a similar amount of damage. Compare these to the cost of a really big earthquake. One estimate, of a magnitude 8.0 or bigger earthquake on the San Andreas fault in Southern California, indicates up to $1 trillion in damages. That's about twenty times the cost of all the other disasters put together! Never mind the thousands of dead and injured, and the massive physical damage—the monetary loss to America would be felt from Maine to Hawaii. No one in America lives far enough away not to feel the effects of such a disaster.

One trillion dollars sounds like a lot of money. Could it really be that much? Let's get an idea of just how big the big one really is. The San Francisco earthquake in 1906 was so strong it ripped the earth for about 200 miles, and the maximum lateral displacement on that tear was measured to be twenty feet. The maximum displacement in the Northridge quake was about two feet. Maybe $1 trillion damage is inflated, but what if it is only $500 billion? Any way you look at it, we should be expecting a huge earthquake, and a huge economic blow.

Let's talk about drugs for a while. The street value of illegal drugs sold in America is estimated to be about $120 billion per year. To put that in perspective, a nuclear-powered aircraft carrier costs about $4 billion. The entire defense budget for a year is currently about $250 billion. When we talk about drugs and related crime, we are talking about some real big bucks! What could some really evil people do with their share of ill-gotten gains when they are measured in the tens of billions of dollars? That much financial power can threaten the existence of whole countries.

When I moved, after graduating from college, I moved deliberately to a small town where, I figured, I could avoid the problems of the big city. It worked—for a while. However, about 1990 a drug dealer moved into a house across the street. I talked to the police, but there wasn't anything they could do without evidence. They did try a drug bust later, but the dealer got rid of his stash too fast and the police ended up going away empty-handed. Finally the landlord discovered the damage the drug dealer and his friends had done to his place and threw them out. Of course, he isn't gone, he's just in someone else's neighborhood. It is estimated that at least 22 million Americans have tried cocaine at least once.

The cost to each of us for losing the war on drugs is already staggering, and we're not through yet, not by a long shot. It is estimated that there are 200,000 gang members in the state of California. There are several countries wishing they had an army that big.

I've heard police officers claim that things are so bad in some neighborhoods that when they get a call regarding a shooting in progress, they make sure they don't get there until after the shooting is over. What's the point? What policeman wants to lose his or her life protecting a neighborhood where the police are considered the enemy? At any moment they can get a bullet in the back of the head, while bystanders cheer. Many police describe their work as low-intensity guerrilla warfare, not police work.

Should we talk about stray plutonium and Russian nuclear scientists for sale to the highest bidder? What if some radical nationalist comes to power in Russia? How about North Korea? Maybe we should save these for a different book.

Even if everything I've just related were not true, there is still one more problem that is so ominous I perceive it to be the most severe of any I worry about. It might seem quite innocuous to some, but I think the implications are so grave, and the impact likely to be so long-lasting, I can't imagine how it can be overstated. That problem is the illegitimate birthrate in America.

I can't think of many things more drastic for America than an explosion in births to young, unwed teenage mothers. According to *U.S. News and World Report,* in 1970 10 percent of the children born in America were born out of wedlock. In 1990, the number was 30 percent. Projections indicate that by the year 2000 the rate may be approximately 40 percent. If the family is torn apart, there is no way to pass a value system on to the next generation. Of all the injustices imposed on African-Americans, the most damaging was undoubtedly the destruction of the family. In over one hundred years, African-Americans, as a group, have never recovered from the damage done to their family structure from slavery; and since the ill-conceived War on Poverty, the situation has actually gotten worse. No portion of the population is expendable; but if the average American family is destroyed, our civilization cannot survive!

How does one generation pass its morals on to the next? Do you think our children will learn how to be responsible parents from watching TV? Do you think that movies will teach them how to resolve problems in a civilized way? Do you think schools will teach children the difference between right and wrong? Will their peers teach them how to be productive adults? It is not impossible to raise good children as a single parent, but the deck is definitely stacked against someone who tries. This problem is even greater among single teenage parents, who usually are unprepared to deal with parenting, either with or without a partner.

Almost every problem I have described will get dramatically worse as a result of an increase in the illegitimate birth rate. An explosion in numbers of welfare recipients, violent crime, drug abuse, and an uneducated work force is on the way. Just about the only thing that can't directly be linked to a sharp increase in the illegitimate birthrate would be an earthquake in California.

The irony of this whole thing is that my two adopted daughters are the result of just such inappropriate behavior. Laurel and I love both of our children, and since our second adoption is an open one, we also know and love the mother of our younger daughter, Michelle. Now that she is a few years older, based on some of the things she has told us and we've seen her do, I am sure that, had she had the chance, she would have lived her youth differently. She suffered a lot of grief and pain she didn't have to, had she only been guided down a different course, instead of the one so many of her friends were following.

A friend of mine has a small business in our town. Recently he was talking with a young unwed mother who had one child and was living on welfare in low-income housing. The young woman was lamenting the position she had put herself in and wishing for a way out. My friend offered her a job. She took the job, and has since become one of his better employees. But all this young mother has received from her neighbors is criticism. "Why did you get a job? You should be home with your baby! If you need more money, why don't you just have another baby? The government will pay." So far she has chosen to follow the harder course, rather than expect someone else to fix her mess. The father has yet to shoulder his responsibility.

Ultimately, that final story is symbolic of our national salvation or destruction. How many people are willing to take responsibility for their own actions? How many expect someone else to solve their problems for them? I don't know. What I *do* know is that we are already going over the cliff. Either we deal with where we are going, or we don't. I am choosing to keep my eyes open.

Chapter 15
It's Not the End of the World

Do you feel drained, completely wiped out? Do you feel as if there is no point reading any further? Are you thinking, *Why not just give up and spend all my money now, before it's too late?* Sure, why not take a trip to the Caribbean and enjoy one last fling before it's all over? If it's really going to be that bad, what good will a budget do? I'm not surprised if you feel that way, but before you do anything rash, let me pursue this with you just a little further.

Would it surprise you if I said that sooner or later you are going to die? Probably not. At the age of seven or eight most people have a pretty good grasp of mortality. You probably knew, at least, that other people die. By the time you became an adult you'd probably lost at least one loved one: a grandparent dying of old age; a friend dying in a car accident. With those experiences, I'm sure, the concept became all too clear. Sooner or later the grim reaper comes for all of us. No exceptions, no exclusions.

In spite of this knowledge of the temporary nature of mortality, the overwhelming majority of us go about our lives, day by day, functioning quite normally. We don't quit our jobs or sit around waiting for the end. We lead healthy, productive lives filled with ups and downs, challenges and triumphs. Many of us even buy life insurance, which should, of course, be called death insurance, and we don't consider that morbid. People buy plots in cemeteries, but we don't consider that indicative of a fascination with death. It is just one of those prudent things that should be taken care of in advance, so that it doesn't cause undue hardship later.

Do you recall anything from the last chapter more profound than dying? If you can accept dying as a normal part of life, and even plan for it, may I suggest that the same is true of living, even if the worst comes true. Unlike dying, we still have a lot of control over how we live, should we choose to exercise it.

Believe it or not, my objective has not been to scare you to death. The last thing I want you to do is freeze with terror, like a deer in the middle of the road at night hit by the headlights of an approaching car. My objective is to motivate you to do something constructive. There may be plenty of time to do just that, *if* you have a plan and carry it out. If you don't have a plan, you are in real trouble.

Many people would prefer not to know. Heads planted firmly in the ground, they feel much better about life. I disagree. I contend that forewarned is forearmed—as long as the information gets transformed into a constructive plan, faithfully executed.

Suppose your taxes doubled, and stayed that way for a decade or two. Would that be the end of the world? Had you prepared to deal with such an eventuality, would it be something you could bear? What if your parents lost half their Social Security payments, and therefore lost their house and had to move in with you, instead of living on their own? With the exception of the last three generations, the concept of elderly parents living with their married children has been seen throughout history. What if your company retirement plan disintegrated? Is it impossible to have a backup?

When I lived in England, in the early 1970s, I found it common for people who lived in small row houses to rent out one of the two bedrooms, including with the rent the occasional use of the kitchen. I know this, of course, because I was one of those renters. If things get bad enough, you may have to do something similar to make your house payments. You may have to start a garden in the back yard. You may have to have the kids get an after-school job to pay for their school clothes. You may not be able to afford to chauffeur the kids around town in a car anymore.

Recently, I had two friends tell me of relatives who'd had their vehicles stolen in Fresno, California, where they happened to live. Police told one of them that one thousand cars are stolen in Fresno each month. The police went on to recommend they *not* use an extra anti-theft device on the car, because it only aggravates the thief. When you do that, they often retaliate for making it hard on them by not only stealing what they want but burning the car as well.

It may get to the point that theft insurance for your car will be so expensive virtually no one will be able to afford it. Cars will never be parked on the street, day or night. When you go to the store, squads of armed guards will roam the walled parking lots to provide the protection necessary to get shoppers to venture out. Also, otherwise law-abiding citizens may regularly break the law by carrying concealed weapons for personal protection without a permit.

Compare that to the accepted custom, a scant hundred-some-odd years ago, of lynching horse thieves after a very short trial held on the spot. We have seen worse. People lived through it. It is not what we would like to see again, and, in fact, it is pathetic. Things could get a lot worse, but they aren't beyond repair. In fact, they never are.

Remember the death of a thousand cuts mentioned in chapter 14? Suppose our elected officials manage to guide the country down a path where they increase the national debt to the maximum the world economy can bear, then just keep us there at the point of maximum pain? They don't add any more massive quantities of debt, nor do they reduce the debt ratio. It could be that there will be no sudden shock, just a very long period of ever more difficult times. That could continue, conceivably, for decades. The analogy of the frog in the pot of water, slowly rising in temperature, fits this scenario perfectly. The crime rate would continue to rise and the standard of living slowly sink. Since no instant in time is particularly worse than the previous one, we slowly, inexorably find ourselves accustomed to being cooked.

But how bad is bad? The invasion of Normandy took place just over fifty years ago. Some of us have relatives or friends still-living who participated in that invasion. Several thousand men didn't live through the day. They knew, that morning, that they might end up lying face down in the surf as the sun set on "the longest day." Yet in spite of that knowledge, they got in the landing craft and prepared to hit the beach and fight the Germans. They had no choice. They knew that the only way to get through the war was to hit it head on.

On Omaha Beach the fighting was particularly bloody. Finally, when the commanding officer came ashore, later in the day, he took one look around at the men huddled behind a stone wall being pounded by artillery and machine-gun fire, and said, in effect, "We've got to get off this beach before we get killed!" He got a crew to blow a hole through the wall with a bungalore torpedo, and his men charged up and off that beach. They lived because they had a plan, and the courage to carry it out.

Now let's put things in perspective. Even the worst interpretation of the last chapter would be a lot less dire for the vast majority of Americans than the invasion of Normandy was. Yes, the financial artillery shells are real, and they can be deadly to your finances. You could find yourself on the street looking for a job, any job, while your family is living in the back of your car. Yes, the financial artillery shells are real, but they are not filled with high explosives. Yet, as in an earlier time, today we have "nothing to fear but fear itself!" Fear that paralyzes us from taking intelligent action to reduce our casualties.

Having your credit cards paid in full will be helpful to you in any situation. If hyper-inflation drives the interest rates over 100 percent, you won't have to worry about the outstanding balance on your credit cards. Owning your own home will be critical for most people under most conditions. Having your car repossessed because you couldn't make the payments will never be helpful. Having food in the house will always be a good idea. None of these courses of action will be counter-productive, even if I am dead wrong and the future is as bright as a field of spring daisies in the morning sunshine.

Suppose I *am* dead wrong! Suppose the next forty years are far better than the last forty. What would be so bad about having your house paid for ten years early? What is so bad about owning the car you drive? Is it really so terrible having money invested for retirement? Wouldn't it be nice to have money in the bank anytime you really need it?

But, if I am right, you're going to need to prepare for the future as if you are going to battle. In the future, your budget may be as important to you as an M16 and a hundred rounds of ammunition are to a foot soldier in combat. Remember—just because there is going to be a fight doesn't mean you're going to be a casualty.

You could definitely say that I have a pessimistic view of the future, but I am not a fatalist. It is true that I can't stop the rain, but I can build a shelter to keep the rain off. My brother put it much better, I think. Eric has served in the army for fifteen years, and I asked him once how he felt about the possibility of being killed in action in some future war. He responded, "Steve, it's like this. I'm not worried about some bullet with 'Lieutenant Johnson' written on it. I'm much more worried about all those millions of bullets flying all over with 'To whom it may concern' inscribed on the side."

Preparation is certainly important in any future I foresee, but preparation is not the only thing that will be necessary. You are going to need courage. The U.S. Army did a study and found that about one in six soldiers exposed to heated combat held onto their rifle and never fired a shot. They further found that fewer than one in one thousand ever took aim at the enemy and pulled the trigger. Instead they fired in the general direction of where the shells were coming from. You must have the courage to convert plans into action if you are to survive a catastrophic financial experience.

By Christmas 1776, General George Washington had been fighting a more or less unsuccessful struggle against a far superior, better trained enemy. As the Revolutionary War dragged on, men deserted by the hundreds; supplies were scarce, and often of poor quality; the winter was cruelly cold to the men living out in the open; the newly formed government succeeded in doing little more than arguing; and with the end of the year only one week off, Washington's army was to go home, having completed their enlistment. The birth of a nation rested on his tired soldiers.

In the dead of winter, instead of giving up and returning to his beloved Virginia and washing his hands of the whole bloody mess, Washington devised a plan. He collected what remained of his battered army—some were wearing rags for shoes—loaded them in tiny boats, and crossed the frozen Delaware to attack the British. He didn't give up; he didn't say "Oh, what's the use." He fought back. He fought the war as best he could with what he had. He took responsibility for himself and his army, and he did the very best he could under extremely difficult conditions.

You, too, may find it an uphill battle. You may spend two years working as hard as you can just to pay off your credit cards. It may seem an impossible goal, just to get out of debt, let alone save for retirement. But don't give up! You must fight on. We are made of better stuff than that. We are a nation of achievers. Many of us have been asleep for too long because it has gotten too easy, but we are not dead yet.

What kind of people leave their homes, sail across the sea, and start a life over in a new, untamed country? What kind of people load all their possessions into covered wagons and travel across the great prairies so they can homestead where they use buffalo dung to build fires? *People who have faith in themselves.* Ofttimes they may have been desperate people, but they turned that desperation into action, not despair.

Think for a moment about one of the most desperate situations in this century. Consider the Jews who were hunted and exterminated by the Nazis during World War II. Think about the young lady and her family who hid from the storm troopers until she was finally captured and killed. How depressing! She never married. She never had any children. She couldn't even live out in the open, only like a caged animal. Nothing is left of that young lady. Nothing except a diary, *The Diary of Anne Frank.*

I think it extremely unlikely that you or I will ever experience a situation as desperate as the Nazi occupation. Certainly we can rise above whatever comes our way. That's not to say it is going to be easy. That's not to say we won't have to put forth our best effort.

Anne Frank and her family did not walk out into the street and turn themselves over to the secret police. They did everything they could to survive. They were careful about every little detail so as not to be found, because that is what was required to survive. And, although it was a supreme struggle, they did it without giving up their humanity. Under such grueling circumstances they came close, but they never gave up. Certainly we can overcome our own comparatively puny challenges, if only we are willing to try hard enough.

Human dignity is not about living the good life. Human dignity is about overcoming difficulties. It is about overcoming. When you learned to walk you probably fell down a thousand times, but you got up and tried a thousand and one. And before you mastered walking, you started to learn to run. It wasn't easy, but you did it anyway. You did whatever it took to overcome that obstacle. You will, most likely, have to draw on that tenacious will in order to win again.

There once was a man with a dream, who wanted to build a new kind of theme park. He took his idea to over one hundred banks in seeking an institution that would back his idea. More than one hundred times he was turned down. At that point, he could have said, "One hundred bankers can't be wrong! It's their job to know a good idea when they see one." Instead, he went to a couple more banks, and he finally found one willing to lend him the venture capital he needed. Walt built his theme park and named it Disneyland. It was a land of dreams, to be sure, but it was built with hard work and faith that any obstacle can be overcome.

Consider a young lady with whom you may be familiar. She was raised in Alabama, the daughter of Captain and Mrs. Keller. They named her Helen. Struck by a childhood disease, she was left blind and deaf. Through the diligent, often agonizing efforts of a certain Miss Sullivan, Helen learned to communicate with the world around her. What had been a swirling fog of chaos and erratic, arbitrary events, became an orderly and comprehensible universe once she learned finger language.

A budget is not likely to make as much difference to you as finger language did to Helen Keller, or sign language to the deaf, but don't underestimate its usefulness, either. Retailers estimate that over 40 percent of sales are impulse purchases. You may make enough money currently to make 40 percent of your purchases on impulse, but may I suggest that you probably won't be able to forever. If you don't believe that 40 percent of your purchases are blindly done on impulse, keep track of what you buy for a while and see. By the way, as you do so, you will be taking a first step toward keeping a budget.

There are two extremes to avoid. Neither makes sense, and both can lead to financial ruin. First, bad things happen! Even now, an amazingly large number of people act as if nothing bad ever happens. Bad things happen, and the chances are they are going to get a lot worse. If you act as if life is a party, you will probably wake the morning after with a hangover. The second extreme is thinking things are going to be so bad that there is no point in trying to prepare. Remember: No matter how hard it gets, someone has had to endure worse and succeeded in doing so. Even though you can't avoid some of life's pitfalls, you don't have to remain on your knees when you fall down. You have a lot under your control, if only you do something about it.

Have faith in yourself. You may be able to do more than you think, if you only put your mind to it. On the other hand, don't be cocky. The challenge ahead is, no doubt, a formidable one. Do all you reasonably can to prepare for what lies ahead.

I have read a couple of books on earthquakes. I have a personal interest in earthquakes, especially earthquakes in California. The San Francisco earthquake of 1906 is most interesting to me, because it is the biggest earthquake to happen in California after large-scale building occurred. It gives a reasonable glimpse at what a really big (magnitude eight or more) earthquake can do. Each book typically has dozens, if not hundreds, of pictures of piles of bricks that used to be houses, shops, hotels, or other structures that failed.

In one book there is a picture of a wooden ranch house north of San Francisco. The brick path leading to the house takes an abrupt jog of about a dozen feet just before it reaches the house. The reason for the jog is that the fault passes right through the garden. Despite its proximity to the deadly earthquake the house suffered little damage, because it was built of resilient material and the foundation was anchored to the ground. No exotic engineering techniques were necessary, just good common sense and a little care.

I think the same is true of our finances. It's not that hard to earthquake-proof your family finances, at least to a significant degree. But if you do what everybody else is doing, you may find yourself buried under a pile of bricks.

Chapter 16
A Few Dollars More

In this book I have encouraged you to avoid debt, and the way I have suggested you do so is by eliminating unnecessary costs. This goes against the knee-jerk reaction of most people who find they have money problems. The obvious solution, to these people, is to earn more money. It may be the obvious solution, but it may not be the smartest. The obvious solution for a deer caught in headlights on a dark road is to hold still so that the approaching car will not see the deer.

If you increase your income, the government takes a larger and larger portion of what you make. If you haven't plugged the holes in your wallet, increasing income to solve your problems is a waste of your time. Yet, having said all that, for some people raising income is exactly the right thing to do. If you're pumping gas, or working nights at a convenience store, you will find it very difficult to ever save enough money to take care of your present needs, let alone the future needs that arise as you grow older.

The way to increase your income with the least amount of risk is simply to work harder. Volunteer for overtime. Show your boss what a hard worker you are and see whether he doesn't remember you at performance review time. This requires no risk on your part, but unfortunately it may also provide the least payback. (If you're flipping burgers at a fast-food joint, you can only work so hard.) Next, you might consider a second job. This may be either for the main bread-winner or the spouse. Be careful! There is a real danger the second job may cost as much money as the second income will produce. For example, if you have children and the wife gets a job to supplement the family income, you could easily end up losing more money than she will make. If you take into account the cost of day care, transportation, clothes, the fact that the second income gets taxed at a higher rate, and the number of times you eat out because everyone is too tired to fix dinner, you might actually find yourself behind financially.

This brings up an issue on which my opinions are definitely not politically correct. But, since I'm not running for any political office, I'm going to speak my mind anyway. If you are offended by what I am about to say, I apologize in advance, but I think the truth speaks for itself, and I won't apologize for that. As a part of the feminist movement, the raising of children has now been labeled one of the lowest, most demeaning jobs a woman can be saddled with. Changing diapers and sitting up with a sick baby may not be fun, but it is a very important duty that must be performed.

Somehow, we have confused prestige and the pursuit of wealth with importance. On that scale, Mother Teresa is a person to be pitied by all because of the grossly demeaning work she has inflicted upon herself. I choose not to pity, but to honor her for reaching out and helping others who need help, rather than being consumed with her own self-importance.

The world doesn't need another corporate president. It doesn't need another millionaire, or even another astronaut. What the world needs is more women who will mother, and more men who will father, and by that I don't mean make more babies. What I mean is, we need more responsible adults willing to raise children to be the kind of people they should be. Being a good parent is a very challenging endeavor; but if parenting is done correctly, the resulting dividends are priceless.

I must add at this point that, in my opinion, any man who is too busy cleaning his rifle or riding his motorcycle to change a messy diaper isn't much of a man. You can hunt bears with a sheath knife, or climb mountains with a broken leg; but, if you haven't stared in the face, a diaper that has exploded and lived to tell about it, you are not a real man. Men, help your wives.

The destruction of the family is not just a phenomenon of the inner city. The teenage birthrate is growing fastest in America among white middle-class suburbans. Parents need to read to their kids. They need to help them with their homework. They need to build things with them in the garage. They need to teach their kids what is right, and what is wrong. They need to know where their kids are, and what they are doing. If both parents are tired from a long day at work, it is all that much harder to meet the challenges of raising a family. I have heard it said that we can't hire enough cops, build enough prisons, or invent enough social programs to replace the parents who have abdicated their responsibility. Don't let the pursuit of prestige and wealth displace the goal of raising good children. Again I must emphasize, this advice is intended for *both* parents.

If you wish to put it in strictly mercenary terms, your children could be your best insurance policy against old age. When you're old and feeble you need children to take care of you, because, let's face it, you won't be able to. Spend the time with them listening to their problems and accomplishments, the way you'd like them to listen to you when you are lonely and filled with arthritis. Patiently help them with their problems, the way you would like others to help you. Raising good, well adjusted, hard working, loving children who care about you is much more important than holding down a second job any way you look at it. If you're smart, you'll think of raising your children as your *first* job and what you do to make money as your second.

A better option than working harder is working smarter. Have you ever tried to shovel more dirt than a back hoe can dig? Nobody is stronger or faster than the machinery we have been able to invent. The way to make more money is to be smarter or more skilled than the competition. You not only have to be smarter, you have to be able to prove it to someone who doesn't know you. In other words, usually you need a diploma. You could earn a degree from a trade school in welding, VCR repair, or as an optometrist's assistant. You could have a degree from a university in chemistry, engineering, nursing, or business. It doesn't matter what it is, as long as the skill is in demand.

When I was in college, during breaks between semesters, I would work as a tire buster in a gas station or automotive center. Had I obtained training as a mechanic, say as a tune-up specialist, I could have doubled my salary. It doesn't have to be a formal education, but somehow you have to be recognized as having a skill that is in demand. I didn't get that training as a tune-up specialist, because I had a different goal in mind. I wanted to be a mechanical engineer, not a car mechanic.

Of course, going to school for years to get a formal education is a struggle, particularly if you are married. It took all the effort I could muster to get through college. I would struggle through as many semesters as I could until I ran out of money. Then I would move back in with my parents and work at a gas station until I'd earned enough money to go back to school. Once I got married the option of living at home was no longer available, so I just stayed in school.

Eventually I borrowed $2,500 to finish my formal education. That was one of the best things I ever did, but I'm glad I didn't go overboard and borrow too much. Many students had it even tougher than I did. Some were married and had little children when they started school. You never in your life saw people more motivated to get good grades.

Another option you might consider is moving into a position of greater responsibility. Good management skills are always rewarded in any organization that knows what it is doing. If you are employed by a company that doesn't reward good work, either from its managers or the rank and file, it must be in the last stages of self-destruction. Find somewhere else to work before the business collapses. Although management may be financially rewarding, it doesn't come without a price. Supervising other workers can be difficult and demanding. You will also probably have to get formal training if you want to develop your leadership skills. It is hard, but going into management can significantly increase your income.

Another option is to work for yourself. This is not for the faint of heart, or for those with the nine-to-five mentality. It is also not for the poorly organized. Ninety-five percent of new small businesses fail in the first five years. This is usually not because they were bad ideas. Typically, these start-up firms fail because of bad business management. What is your cash flow? How much merchandise should you keep on hand? How should you handle employees who don't work hard? How can you advertise most effectively? How much profit should you take out of the company without depleting the working capital? How do you handle taxes? Small business is truly the lifeblood of the American economy, but those who venture forward and succeed are neither the timid or weak.

Invest in yourself. It's probably one of the best investments you will ever make. Keep learning your whole life. Night school is an option many people take. Make the sacrifice to get ahead early; then you will get out of first gear and start going somewhere. The longer you wait, the harder it gets and the less time you have left to get a return on your investment—so start early.

When I was young, I bought toys with the money I earned. I didn't need to save money, except to buy toys, since all my needs were taken care of by my parents. I am no longer small, and I have to take care of other people's needs now so that they don't have to worry. I still have toys, but they are no longer a central part of my life.

You have often heard, and in a sense it is true, that no amount of money can compensate for a person's life. It is an intrinsic, ingrained part of Western thought that we, as individuals, would go to extreme lengths to save the life of even a single person in danger. However, that is, in a very real sense, absolute romantic hogwash! Every day, millions of people climb out of bed in the morning and willingly exchange another day of their lives for a few lousy bucks.

You have often heard that time is money. Time is, among other things, what we use to measure the passage of life with. When we work, we trade a small portion of our life, one day at a time, in exchange for money. We do this of our own free will, knowing full well that we have only so many days in our lives. We exchange our lives for money. Everybody needs a place to stay, and food to eat, though most of us go far beyond that in our pursuit of material possessions.

My father put it this way: He pointed out that my scoutmaster was giving his life for the scouts in our troop, just as surely as if he were throwing his body on top of a hand grenade. He would spend his Tuesday evenings, his weekends, and his summer vacations giving us the Boy Scout program. My father said we ought to be grateful for the time our scoutmaster and others gave, because they were never going to get that time back again. It was gone—forever.

Every day, we give up a little of our life in exchange for whatever we get in return. Don't waste your life. If you need more money, work for it. If you think you will need money in the future, save for it. If you don't need more money, do something else with your time. When you spend your money, you are really spending your life. Don't exchange your life for a pile of silly gadgets and fluff. Buy only the things that are really worth the time you sacrificed to get them. Be sure you spend your time wisely on that which is of lasting worth. What are *you* going to give your life for?

Chapter 17
Just to Be Sure

A long time ago, I was told about a man who seemed to have everything anybody ever needed, and plenty more. He had a very large home and many nice things, including new cars and a boat. His wife and kids wore new clothes, and they went nice places. Though only in his forties he was, to all outward appearances, financially set. Then suddenly, without warning, his wife found herself a widow.

I'm sure having a fatal heart attack wasn't listed in his daily planner. Some things come whether we are ready or not. He was an intelligent man, obviously successful in his profession, but apparently he'd never seriously considered the possibility that death would come for him before he was old.

The person who told me the story had been called upon to assist the family in their unfortunate situation. What the neighbors could not tell, as they drove past their house with the nice cars and the boat parked in the driveway, was that the deceased owned very little of all that neat stuff. The house had a big mortgage. The cars and boat had been bought with credit, as had many of the other things that filled their house. Once the estate had been settled, and the creditors paid off, the mother found herself virtually penniless. Here she was, the mother of several small children, with no money, and faced with the prospect of having to start all over again, alone.

Had he considered seriously the fact he might not live as long as most people do, he would have done things much differently. Maybe he would have put off buying the boat until the home loan was further along. Maybe he would have driven the same car longer, until it was paid for, instead of buying a new one each year. I'm sure there were many other things he would have done, but he figured, probably, he would simply take care of them later. Perhaps he could have, but he never got the chance.

One of the things he should have done was to have a life insurance policy of sufficient size to provide for his family in the event of his untimely death. Had he paid for most things with cash and had a reasonably good-sized life insurance policy, he could have left enough money so that his wife would not have had to throw herself on the mercy of friends, relatives, and charities. Suppose the only debt he'd had was his home, and that it had been half paid for. Let's also assume the house wasn't a lavish palace, but simply a house sufficient for his family's needs. Let's further assume that he had a term life insurance policy of three times the value of his yearly salary. His wife could have paid off the home loan, invested the rest in conservative mutual funds, and if she had a job, any job, she could have gotten by on what she made.

In my opinion this is the bare minimum you should consider, but many people don't even do that. If you want the wife to be able to stay home and just live off the dividends, then you will need much more. It needs to be about ten times the husband's yearly salary. In order to have a relatively constant income of $30,000 while allowing for the principal to increase to keep up with inflation, you need somewhere in the neighborhood of $500,000 to $600,000 intelligently invested in stocks and bonds.

Of course, certain expenses will go away if the father dies—for example, you won't need two cars anymore, and the house will be paid for—but new ones may appear. Ten times your yearly salary is a lot of insurance to pay for. For most people, that much insurance is simply out of the question. Sometimes you can get a special deal through a professional organization. If you have some special offer, it may be too good to pass up.

I mentioned term insurance. Generally speaking, there are two types of insurance. Term is one type, whole life the other. There are really many variations and names for various schemes, but for our purposes we'll simplify it down to these two types. Term insurance is what you usually think of when you think of insurance. You purchase a policy by paying a small amount each month. If the insured person dies, the insurance company pays the beneficiaries the agreed-upon amount. That is all there is to it.

Whole-life insurance is really a scheme where a savings account is added to an insurance policy. If you live past some specific age, you get the accrued value. Sometimes it is repaid to the beneficiaries over a period of time as an annuity. As you may have guessed, whole-life policies are more expensive than term insurance policies, often much more expensive. In fact, they are usually much more expensive than a comparable term insurance policy and a separate savings plan. By investing the money yourself, you may be able to retire with two or three times the nest egg you would have with a whole-life insurance policy. Figure out the difference for yourself. Do your homework. There is a simple rule of thumb for figuring interest. It is sometimes referred to as the rule of seventy-two. Basically, the rule goes like this: Seventy-two divided by the yearly interest rate will give you the number of years required to double your money. Put another way, the yearly interest rate times the number of years to double your money will equal seventy-two. Therefore, if you have some money invested at 7.2 percent interest, the investment will double in about ten years. At 14.4 percent it will double in about five years. It is only a rule of thumb, but it is very useful.

For some, whole life is the way to go, because without it they wouldn't save for retirement at all. I firmly believe there is no reason you can't build a nest egg of your own, yet many people lack the discipline to do it. If that is the case for you, go with whole life. No matter what you do, be sure you have insurance *and* investments.

So who should you insure? Insurance is not a measure of a person's worth; it is a means of replacing the income or essential services that a person was providing the family. When we were first married and had no children, I had no insurance on my wife. That doesn't mean she wasn't worth anything; it's just that snuggling up to all those dollar bills seemed like a poor substitute for a wife. If we'd had small children, I would have had to seriously consider the cost of child care. By the time we had children I wasn't too worried about it, though maybe I should have been. Ask yourself how much money it would require to replace the essential services that each person brings to the family before you decide if (or how much) insurance you should have for each person.

One of the best forms of insurance a family can have is for the wife to have a marketable skill that she can draw on in the event she finds herself without a husband. Unfortunately, all too often these days women find themselves without a husband, without the husband even dying. Even though I recommend that the wife spend a lot of time with the kids, so that they can learn what parents do, it would almost be foolhardy for a woman simply to assume she can always depend on her husband's income being there. Making sure that all these needs are met involves some difficult family matters, and they will certainly require some sacrifice on the part of all the family members. Just be sure you don't forget what your core family values are, and don't get caught up in the pursuit of status or wealth.

What if both spouses are working and there aren't any children? What is the insurance for? You could have a policy to cover funeral costs, but on the other hand, suppose you simply saved for that eventuality? If you pay on a policy for several years, you can bet that eventually the company will recover more than they will pay out. Sooner or later everybody dies. The insurance companies know it, and they price their policies accordingly so that they make a sizable profit.

When you reach the age of about fifty you will find that the cost of term insurance begins to get outrageously expensive. This is not age discrimination; old people die. Not surprisingly, the older you get, statistically speaking, the more likely you are to die in the immediate future. By the time you turn fifty-five or sixty, two things should have happened: your kids should have moved away, or be about to, and you should have saved enough to retire. If you have, then whether you live or die you should not have to worry about your family's financial welfare. For most people, it makes sense to cancel life insurance upon retirement.

Don't forget to get a will or a living trust. A few hundred dollars spent on a straightforward will could save your children a lot of effort and a significant loss of money. Keep it simple, too. This is one time I would recommend the help of a professional. Do-it-yourself law could be more risky than hang-gliding in a lightning storm.

I have never had life insurance on any of my children, for the same reason that I have never had any on my wife. Financially, they need me; to me, they are a financial burden. Remember, insurance is not a measure of a person's personal worth. It is only a monetary safeguard to mitigate the serious financial consequences of losing a family member. Besides Mindy and Michelle, we had one other daughter, Christina, whom I have not yet mentioned in this book. She died of an incurable, inherited disease just before her first birthday. It was not cheap to pay for the expenses directly related to her death, but it wasn't outrageous, either. I had enough savings to cover the cost of the funeral and burial. The big costs were piling up long before she died.

This brings me to the subject of medical insurance. By the time you read this the rules of the game may have changed radically, based on the health-care debates that raged recently in Washington. If some form of broad-based universal coverage reemerges and is legislated, I recommend you hurry and buy more food storage. If something massive is passed and signed into law, every one of us will be in a lot of financial trouble, even sooner than we would otherwise have been. Keep in mind one fact: The institution that recently has been telling us it can provide for everybody and keep medical costs the same, or even reduce them, is the same institution that told Native Americans the land would be theirs for as long as the rivers flowed, the grass grew, and the sky provided rain. The faces may have changed over the last hundred and fifty years, but the line hasn't changed much.

You know they have to be lying because doctors keep inventing new medical treatments. Medical costs have to increase faster than the rate of inflation for as long as medical research continues. They are inventing new ways of meeting medical needs every day. You didn't need an ultrasound or a CAT scan thirty years ago, because they hadn't been invented yet. Now you need them. Since matters of life and death are so emotionally charged, and because the government is so bad at saying "no" to entitlement programs, the cost has to explode unless they artificially limit the treatments available. Watch for this one to be the log, not straw, that broke the camel's back.

But for the moment, let's assume things stay the same. Medical insurance that covers every little "owie" is very expensive compared to insurance that has a deductible. The real utility of medical insurance is to cover the big ones. When Christina was critically ill, it cost us a total of about $6,000 for her direct medical expenses over two calendar years. That sounds like a lot of money, but we didn't really have much trouble handling it because we'd saved for the unexpected. Compare that to the $40,000 to $50,000 had we not been insured. Had her illness been more prolonged, or had more expensive treatments been available, it could as easily have cost $500,000! That is what insurance is for. Thankfully it doesn't happen very often. If it did, however, that would be enough to take my marker off the board for the duration of the game. If you are paying for the bulk of the premiums, buy insurance with a reasonable deductible and pay for the little ones as they come. Again, do your homework; compare.

If you lost your home, that would also be catastrophic. Homeowners are usually required to carry a standard coverage for the duration of the loan on their home. Never consider dropping it just because the loan is paid off. You need that coverage more than the bank does. Make sure that you have sufficient coverage for the current value of your home and its contents, in your location, after considering the disasters that could possibly happen to you. Most of all, make sure you are covered against someone tripping on the front sidewalk. A lawsuit may be the most expensive and most likely disaster you will ever encounter.

It is interesting to note that most policies expressly do not cover damage as a result of war, revolution, or other civil disturbance. This explains why certain people took such a dim view of other people looting or burning their stores during the L.A. riots. A person could get really upset watching a lifetime's work disappear in an afternoon at the hands of total strangers.

Car insurance is an interesting one to consider. There are two things that can go wrong. The first is that your car can be wrecked. If your car is worth a lot, the coverage is more expensive; if it is not, the cost is less. No big surprise so far. This is, of course, a consideration when buying a car. The more expensive a car is, the more expensive it is to insure. Regardless of how expensive the car is, there is a limit to how much damage can be done to it, barring the possibility that it is a priceless collector's item. If you have such a car, leave it home and drive a Chevy or a Ford.

There is another consideration. The amount of damage you do driving a car is theoretically unlimited! Imagine driving down the road; you swerve suddenly to avoid a ball that bounces out into the street, and your car hits the rear of a parked car. The parked car happens to be a 1914 Stutz Bearcat. Immediately a famous personal-defense lawyer staggers out of the driver's side of the car exclaiming, "My back! My back!" as he carefully writes down your license plate number between grunts and groans.

If you have $50,000 in liability insurance and you get hit with a law suit for $5,000,000, the insurance company may just say, "Oh well," and let you pay off the $4,950,000 that is your share. But if you have coverage for $500,000 they will be much more likely to get in there and fight on your behalf, since they stand to lose a lot more. The bottom line is this: What you are really getting with your insurance is a hired gun, and they're a lot more likely to get a really fast draw to protect their $500,000 share than $50,000. The fact that it may cost only 20 percent more to get the $500,000 rather than the $50,000 makes it well worth the expense.

I think credit-card insurance is more or less a waste. The most you can be charged if you are responsible and report stolen or lost credit cards is $50 each. If your cards get lost or stolen more often than once every five years it may be a good deal, but otherwise you should consider just being careful and not leaving them where they can sprout legs and walk; you decide.

Mortgage insurance is another redundant form of insurance, as far as I am concerned. In the event of my death, my wife would use part of my life insurance to pay off the house. I don't need a separate policy to handle my mortgage. I just include it in my calculation of my life insurance policy.

Ultimately the question comes down to, "How much insurance should I buy?" That question reminds me of the original *Star Trek* TV series, which was popular in the 1960s when I was a teenager. Mr. Spock, who was only half human, always clearly defined the answer in cold, relentlessly logical terms. Dr. McCoy inevitably responded with pure passion, devoid of logic. Kirk, the captain, drew from these two and added his own trademark character trait, courage. Kirk also had more than his fair share of good luck.

The simple answer to the question, How much insurance should I buy? is, As much as you can afford, but no more than you need. If you think about it, that is a ridiculous answer—you will never know how much insurance you really need until it is too late. The real answer to the question depends on a character trait that the original *Star Trek* neglected to portray in any of its characters: wisdom. Wisdom is a difficult personal quality to attain; but, to those who do attain it, the rewards are great. If you develop wisdom, many of your financial problems will simply fade away.

Chapter 18
One Last Check

A good family friend found herself in a real financial mess after she'd divorced her husband. She had not been excluded from the family finances before the divorce, but she was not included, either. She had been on her own for about six months, with four children to support, when all of a sudden all her checks started to bounce. Without a clue as to how to find the cause of her problem, she went to the bank and asked for help. They asked to see the last bank statement she had balanced. A sheepish smile crept across her face. "Balanced?" she asked. "Statement that I have balanced?" After a moment's hesitation she admitted she, personally, had never actually balanced a statement. In fact, she admitted, most of them were still in the envelope unopened. She really had no idea how to balance a checkbook.

The bank graciously offered to straighten out her checkbook if she would bring in the statements. The next day she returned to the bank. The statements were all balanced and the error found. She had inadvertently entered in her checkbook the same deposit twice, which caused her to think she had more money in her account than she actually had. The bank could see she'd made an honest mistake. They offered to erase the bad-check charges if she would bring her account up to the minimum balance. She was so delighted at the understanding attitude of the bank that she immediately responded, "Oh, thank you so much! Here, let me write you a check right now," as she reached for her checkbook. "You should have seen the look on the face of the lady behind the desk!" my friend laughed as she told me the story.

She has since become quite proficient at balancing a checkbook. However, an astounding number of people have not mastered this concept. I know someone who works as a pharmacist, who relates the following experience: A person came into the pharmacy fuming mad. "What do you mean my check is no good?! Look at this. I have a whole book of checks! I've got a whole box of them at home! What do you mean, my check is no good?!" The pharmacist was unable to explain.

Handling a checking account is, to the modern era, what the facts of life were to the Victorian Age: They were never explained to the young; it was simply assumed that, somehow or other, they would figure things out on their own, when they got older. It may be that parents don't explain checking to their children today for the same reason that parents didn't explain the facts of life to their children then. Perhaps they don't know much about the subject and feel embarrassed about displaying their ignorance. For those of you who wondered, but didn't know who to ask, I will now explain the facts of . . . checking.

A check is an IOU. It is simply a promise to pay a specified amount of legal currency to a specific person or entity. It is written on preprinted paper to prevent the altering of information on the check. In order for a check to be valid, an amount equal to or greater than the amount written on the check must be in the account *before* the check is written. It is against the law to write a check knowing that there are insufficient funds deposited in the account to cover the check. It is a law that is flagrantly and blatantly broken and is seldom enforced to the full extent allowed by statute.

However, those who push their luck too far occasionally find themselves in jail for a long time.

Every time you write a check, the value of the check is subtracted from your account. When all the money in your account has been removed by cashing checks, no more checks may be written until more money has been added to the account. New money, cash, *dinero*—not a check from your account, which is empty. The number of checks in your checkbook has nothing to do with how much money is in your account.

Balancing your account is really quite simple. All you do is add to the checkbook total everything the bank doesn't know about yet or that you didn't know about until you got your statement. When the totals match, you're done. Study the example shown at the back of this chapter as you read the text.

First, open your bank statement and examine it carefully. Notice that somewhere on the statement it has a list of the checks that have been returned to the bank. That money has now left your account. Find the highest check number listed on your bank statement. Find the same check number in your checkbook and draw a line below the total associated with that check. Write that total from your checkbook in the margin of your bank statement. Do this where you have a little room to work. Now, go through your checkbook and make a small mark next to each check number that matches the checks on the statement, to show which checks have cleared the bank this month.

A few checks above the line will *not* have a mark next to them. These outstanding checks are subtracted from your checkbook, but the bank has not subtracted them because it has not yet received them. *Add* them back to your total written in the margin of the statement. Put the check number next to each dollar value, so you can go back and verify your work later. If you have deposits on your statement that are listed below the line in your checkbook, *add* those to your total in the margin also. If the bank has paid interest, *add* that to your checkbook and to the total in the margin. Notice that you are *adding* to your total from your book to make it match the total on the statement. There is one exception. If there are any bank charges, *subtract* them from the checkbook and the total in the margin.

The total in the margin should now equal the total on the statement. If it doesn't, go back and look at your math. Start with the numbers in the margin, then look to see if your checkbook adds up. Usually the problem results from carelessness, such as adding a check or subtracting a deposit in your checkbook. But if you are careful, you will find that it goes fairly smoothly after you get the hang of it. It isn't that hard once you work at it for a while. My mother had trouble with math for years. When her teacher in school asked her what she would have if she added three apples to two bananas, she'd answer, "fruit salad." Her teacher gave her a passing grade if she promised to go away and never come back. But even my mother learned how to balance a checkbook; in fact, she taught me how to do it.

If you have troubles, write the fewest checks possible, so you can keep the statement simple. Use cash instead of checks whenever possible. (That isn't a bad habit, anyway.) *Never* take checks out of order; you will never make sense of your statement if you do. Maybe each spouse should have his/her own checkbook and separate accounts. Always keep a positive balance in your checkbook. You can't mint money; you are not the government! Never use those check-guarantee programs, which just roll your bad checks into a loan. They are the kiss of death.

It may seem like a bother to balance your checkbook, but it is more important than brushing your teeth each morning.

If you do it regularly, every month, it will take you less than the total time you spend brushing your teeth, too. And, if you do both, not only will you be able to smile without being embarrassed, you will also have something to smile about.

Bank Statement

FIRST NATIONAL BANK OF
PONGO PONGO

Balance at beginning of period			$1,500.00
1 Dec.	Draft 11	-200.00	$1,300.00
8 Dec.	Draft 13	-50.00	$1,250.00
15 Dec.	Draft 12	-100.00	$1,150.00
18 Dec.	Draft 14	-300.00	$850.00
19 Dec.	Deposit	800.00	$1,650.00
23 Dec.	Draft 16	-75.00	$1,575.00
Balance at end of period			$1,575.00

Item	Amount	Item	Amount
11✓	$200.00	14✓	$300.00
12✓	$100.00	16✓	$75.00
13✓	$50.00		

Handwritten annotations: $1,325.00 ← / +$250.00 #15 / $1,575.00

Check Book

Date	Check#	Withdrawals Deposits	Total
			1,500.00
28 Nov. 1995	11✓	-200.00	-200.00
			1,300.00
5 Dec. 1995	12✓	-100.00	-100.00
			1,200.00
6 Dec. 1995	13✓	-50.00	-50.00
			1,150.00
14 Dec. 1995	14✓	-300.00	-300.00
			850.00
14 Dec. 1995	15	-250.00	-250.00
			600.00
19 Dec. 1995	Deposit	800.00	800.00
			1,400.00
20 Dec. 1995	16✓	-75.00	-75.00
			1,325.00

Handwritten: ok

Chapter 19
Try Me One More Time

"Excuse me for sounding dumb, but I still have a few questions about keeping a budget. You make it sound so simple, and we have started a budget, as you suggested, but there are some things I just don't seem to understand."

"Well, ask me some questions; I'll do my best to answer them. I don't have answers for everything. Sometimes, you will invent solutions that work better for you than anything anybody else could think up. But go ahead and ask, and I'll do my best."

"I don't understand why just keeping track of what I spend solves my money problems. If I keep a budget, my house payment doesn't go down. Why do you make such a big deal about writing everything down?"

"Your house payment won't go down, that is true. Just writing everything down won't give you the control you need, either. Remember, a damage assessment is not a budget. A budget allots a certain amount of money for each group of things you buy. The point is, you are buying a lot of things you don't need. You don't have any handle on them until you keep a budget. Once you keep a budget, you can start to make specific comparisons that you couldn't before.

"I knew someone who lived by his budget religiously. He took his family on a vacation; and when they returned, they took a vacation from their budget for about a week.

Suddenly they found they had spent two hundred dollars they had not planned on spending. A budget works only if you use it to make decisions about whether or not you're going to buy a certain item. After a while you will think about buying something but you will not buy it, or you will put it off until later, because you know the category it comes under has insufficient funds. That's how it keeps you from spending money you don't have."

"All right, what do I do with the money that is left over in the category at the end of the month? Do I transfer it over into my savings account?"

"You could say it is already in a savings account. Whatever is left in the Car category is being saved for car repairs, or could be used eventually to buy a car to replace the one you are now driving. As the House category gets larger, you are saving for a new roof. Just leave it there and let it increase in value until you need it."

"I don't understand which money is which. Is my car money in my checking account or my savings account?"

"My checking account, my savings account, and the money on the dresser are all part of one big whole. When I spend it, then it becomes a specific kind of money as I write it down in my budget. I also have some bank accounts and mutual funds reserved for retirement, and two others for the kids' college. *That* money is not used for any reason until it is time to do so. These are separate, and each is a kind of category, although I don't show them in my budget. They are not a part of my budget, because they are dormant until I retire, or my kids go to college. Until that time, no money can be retrieved from any of these accounts.

"There are many other ways to do this. Some people actually keep a different envelope for each category. I find that a clumsy way to do it, but maybe you will find it a useful way to get started. Some people use a checkbook for some things and their bank account for others. If it meets your needs, that's fine. Just be sure that money in, minus money out, equals money saved."

"What do you do with interest earned from your bank accounts?"

"I ignore it for the time being. The retirement accounts are the ones that are making the big bucks, and I just roll the interest over in the account for the present. The checking and passbook accounts make a little money, but I just allow it to accumulate as if it were not there. Occasionally I forget to write something down, or I lose the receipt. Because this is rare, the interest will more than make up for the occasional mistake. The difference results in a small hidden savings account. It doesn't amount to much but it doesn't hurt, either."

"We get paid every two weeks, but we budget by the month. What do we do with the two extra paychecks each year?"

"One check I put into Car and the other I put into Savings. You do what you want with yours. Maybe, at first, you will put it all toward paying off debts. Later, Savings should be the obvious choice."

"What category would you take furniture out of?"

"Suppose I decided that our family needed a new chair for the living room. First, I might suggest that it should come out of House. Suppose that Laurel says we need to save for a new roof and we can't afford to take anything out of House right now. Since we disagree, and that category is not my personal category, I need to find a different source of money. Then I might say that we should split it between Wife and Husband. If she agrees, it's a done deal. If she says no, because she is saving for the kids' books and Christmas, then I can always subtract the whole thing from Husband. If there isn't enough, and I still want it, I will just have to wait until

I have enough in Husband to afford to buy it. Don't use emergency money for a purchase like this. You can get by for a while without a chair. Save emergency funds for the real emergencies."

"Should I include the money I expect to get from a court settlement in a couple of months? I know it's going to be settled; the money just isn't here yet."

"You remind me of the fisherman who was asked how many fish he had caught. He responded that as soon as he had this one and two more, he would have three. Don't count your chickens until they hatch—you may find a dinosaur egg in the nest."

"You haven't said anything about using a computer. Many people use a computer to manage their money. Do you recommend it?"

"Let's put it this way. A computer and software, which will both become hopelessly obsolete in a few years, will cost you at least $1,500. A spiral binder will cost about $1. Why do you suppose I'm not crazy about the computer option? If you already have a computer, and you want to spend the money for the software, a computer can do a marvelous job of tracking your expenses. But you don't need it! A computer is overkill, but it can be fun. I'll let you decide which way is best for you. Personally, even though I have a computer, I prefer the spiral binder."

"What do you do if they don't give you a receipt?"

"When I go on official travel, I keep a 3 X 5 card in my pocket or wallet and write things down as I go. When I buy a meal in a restaurant with several other people I often don't get a receipt. In other words, I make my own receipt. When I get home I write it down in my budget."

"Thank you very much. I think I understand better now."

"You're welcome. It's been my pleasure. I think that

once you get going you'll find it isn't hard. Something I never thought of will come up, unique to your family. Invent a solution and keep going. I wish you the best. Good luck."

Chapter 20
Flight Plan

The twin-engine Cessna pulled off the connecting tarmac onto the massive runway. The pilot glanced sideways for a moment out of the port window at the north side of the LAX terminal complex, then returned his eyes to the runway before him. It was big enough for the world's largest aircraft to take off. The two turbo-prop engines buffeted the small plane as they strained like caged animals. Finally the brakes were released, and the plane sped down the runway. The craft quickly increased speed until the nose wheel lifted up and the plane rotated back. Then the rear wheels left the concrete and she was free of the ground. The plane was at cruising speed and altitude in less than ten minutes, heading into the setting sun over the shimmering Pacific.

"I love the sunset over the ocean, don't you? Say, how is that altimeter working?"

"It seems fine, why?"

"It acts up on occasion. So, how do you like that sunset?"

"Oh, it's beautiful. What do you mean, acts up?"

"Well, it usually works fine, but sometimes it just kind of sticks. You may be slowly changing altitude, but according to the altimeter you can't tell. You know, when the sun sets like this—with clouds forming at the higher altitudes and fog coming off the surface of the ocean—it's magnificent! Look how the sun is reflected off the clouds above and the fog below. The world just seems to stand still for a moment."

"Yeah, yeah, the sunset's great. Tell me more about the altimeter. If your altimeter doesn't work sometimes, how do you know how high you are?"

"Usually I just look out the window at the ground and I can guess about how high I am. You know about how big a car or a house is, so it isn't that hard to tell how high we are. You know, I think when the sun has just barely set and the clouds turn the color of deep red, about the way they have right now, things could hardly look prettier. The color seems to transform everything, including the plane."

"I don't see any cars. I can't see any houses, either!"

"Of course you can't. We're over the ocean. Besides, the fog is covering the ocean anyway. Say, would you say that the artificial horizon is parallel with the sunset?"

"What do you mean?"

"It seems like that gauge is about ten degrees counter-clockwise to the world. Does it look that way to you?"

"Wait a minute! First the altimeter doesn't work, and now you tell me that the artificial horizon doesn't know up from down! What *does* work on this plane? Here we are flying off into the night, and all our instruments can't be trusted. Are you going to ask me to go out on the wing with a stick to see if there is gas in the tanks?"

"You know what your problem is?"

"No! What?"

"You need to loosen up. Look at you. You're about to have a nervous breakdown. You could have a heart attack. It's not good for you to be so nervous. It will take five years off your life if you don't relax a little."

"Five years! Five years! If this altimeter of yours doesn't work right, I could lose *fifty* years off my life tonight!"

"Don't worry. I know where I'm going. I'm going due west."

"How do you know? Maybe the compass is loused up too."

"Doesn't matter. I have a better compass than any plane ever had."

"Oh, really. What's that?"

"The sun! As long as they haven't rearranged the solar system, I know I have to be heading almost exactly due west. That glow up ahead is a sunset, and that has to be in the west."

"Well, that's just great! I feel a lot better! I feel so wonderful now that I know we are going due west. There are just two things wrong with this situation that may have escaped your notice."

"What're they?"

"First, if I'm not mistaken, is that sun setting, or does the sun just stay on the horizon on the planet you come from?"

"Oh, we're getting ugly now!"

"You could say that. Then there is the other problem."

"What other problem?"

"I thought San Francisco was more or less north. I'm new at this flying stuff. Maybe it is standard operating procedure to travel west first, then take a right turn and go straight north. I was under the impression that most planes kind of mixed the two and took the shortest path between two points."

"*San Francisco?* I thought you wanted to go to *San Diego.* I just figured we would enjoy a little flying on the way there and take a little detour."

"Would you do me a little favor?"

"What's that?"

"Next time we go flying together, would you mind filing

a flight plan? And one other thing—would you mind doing it *before* we leave the ground?"

Chapter 21
Of Kings and Nations

Ever found yourself owing so much on credit cards, the car, and doctor bills you had to sell the wedding ring for less than a quarter of what you paid for it? You might take solace in knowing the same thing happened to Napoleon Bonaparte. Consider, for a moment, how history might have been different if France had not sold the Louisiana Territory for four cents per acre. Nations are subject to the same economic conditions and pressures; they even fall victim to the same enticements that tempt individuals. Had Napoleon not embarked on building an empire with costly European wars, he would not have had to sell the Louisiana Territory to pay for his military ventures. Vanity is a terrible master.

Consider Germany's Weimar Republic. At the beginning of the twentieth century, Germany wanted to keep up with the Joneses (i.e., Britain and France), who had colonies the world over. Germany had relatively few colonies as a result of unification in the latter part of the nineteenth century—a late starter, compared to its rivals. World War I was a result of this and other factors, and in the end Germany, having lost, was saddled not only with its own war debt but that of the Allied nations as well. Nations don't declare bankruptcy, generally, so Germany did the next best thing: It printed enough money to pay off the war debt, thus destroying its economy in the process. Hyper-inflation and mass unemployment resulted, setting the stage for Adolf Hitler to crawl out of a back alley and seize power.

Money, or the lack of it, has had a profound effect on world history, and this is bound to continue as long as nations exist. Nations are run by people, and people make judgments, both good and bad. The only difference is that individuals usually affect only a few, perhaps a handful of people. Heads of state routinely make decisions that, for better or worse, affect millions. The Marshall Plan, instituted after World War II, may well have saved several Western European nations from the slavery and sorrow that would have resulted from Communist domination. In my book, a free Western Europe is a bargain, at any price. But it was made possible only because the United States had the necessary financial resources.

No doubt many factors contributed to the collapse of the Soviet empire in 1991. I am convinced, however, that the inability of the USSR to compete with the economies of the capitalist West, as well as Communism's failure to provide a reasonable standard of living for its people, played major parts. It finally became apparent to the Soviet leadership that they must change their ideology and dogma. They tried to provide a soft landing both for themselves and their country as they endeavored to reform the Soviet Union. It was, undoubtably, less bloody than it might have been, but it certainly did not follow a well-choreographed script.

It seemed to me much like the motorcyclist who crossed the finish line of the race with his fingertips on the wide-open throttle, his chin on the back of the seat, and the toes of both his boots dragging on the ground four feet behind the rear wheel. As he passed the checkered flag he yelled, "Give me just a moment; I seem to be having a little difficulty." When you think back on it, isn't it amazing that a country that was so powerful and that had changed so little politically in three-quarters of a century could crumble almost overnight? I'm sure many Russians swore it would never happen.

When I came back from England in 1974, I was amazed to see lines of cars around American gas stations. Rationing? Even-numbered license plates on even days, and odd plates on odd days? I'd never seen anything like it in all my life, and, since World War II, neither had anybody else. As a result of conflict with Israel, the Arab states, along with the other members of the OPEC cartel, punished the West for supporting Israel. They both cut the world oil supply and dramatically increased the price of oil. Not only did this carry a political message to the intended target, it didn't hurt the oil suppliers financially, either.

The eventual result should have been predictable, but OPEC seemed not to see it coming. They pushed their advantage too far. Ultimately the price of oil reached such a high level that it became more economically practical to get oil from a turnip. Oil was found almost everywhere, even in the treacherous North Sea. Never would it have been profitable to drill in such adverse conditions at the preembargo prices. Not only that, but cars and other devices powered by oil derivatives were reengineered, at a cost of billions, to make them more efficient, thus further tipping the balance of supply and demand. Eventually, OPEC lost control of the market because there were too many players, and the price of oil fell again.

When Iraq invaded Kuwait in 1990, I heard several opinions about what it all meant. International conspiracy; no blood for oil; Saddam Hussein had been brought to power by the CIA; there are atrocities all over the world—why defend a bunch of ragheads, anyway? Through all the flurry and slogans I heard, one explanation made the most sense to me: Saddam Hussein sent his armies into Kuwait for the same reason Willie Sutton said he robbed banks—because that's where the money is. The United States government sent eight aircraft carriers, hundreds of aircraft, thousands of tanks, and 500,000 men half way around the world for the same reason they sent marshals after Jesse James: The government doesn't like people robbing the banks that U.S. citizens depend on.

Iraq had just fought a very expensive eight-year war with Iran, which had yielded very little in return. Iraq had borrowed billions of dollars from other Gulf states, including Kuwait and Saudi Arabia. The other Gulf states were not too enchanted with the radical fundamentalist movement in Iran, and if Iraq could keep Iran in line, they were more than happy to make a little loan to Iraq. What Iraq hoped to gain from war with Iran was the capture of some critical real estate on the Gulf, including the port facilities necessary to load oil tankers. When the war didn't work out, Saddam Hussein wanted the loans forgiven. The bank refused, so Saddam took over the bank.

The Kuwaitees should have done a better job of protecting the bank. Their army was little more than a speed bump against the massive, battle-tested Iraqi army. Undoubtably, they believed the myths of Arab brotherhood that had sounded so nice. When a nation is as rich as Kuwait is, they shouldn't be so trusting and simply assume their neighbors will play by the rules. Fortunately for Kuwait, we needed their oil desperately enough to reconquer their country for them. If there is one thing America is more addicted to than drugs, it is a lifestyle dependent on cheap energy. If that offends our sensibilities perhaps we should change our lifestyle, instead of putting ourselves in such a situation again.

Other commodities are subject to supply and demand as well. Inflation rocked Europe after the discovery of the Americas by Spain and Portugal. That seems impossible to comprehend, since the coinage was gold and silver, the standard by which we usually measure everything else. The plunder of the New World included mountains of gold and silver, which was dumped on the world market with no appreciable increase in the amount of goods and services. Since the total number of goods and services did not increase but the amount of available gold and silver did, people simply spent greater amounts of gold and silver to purchase the same amount of goods. This produced the result that is as predictable as rain in the tropics: inflation.

One of the more intriguing little conspiracies in recent history begins with World War II. Great Britain had been pounded by the war, and not just physically. Sustaining the war effort had proven tremendously expensive, and England came out of the war a crippled soldier. Between 1946 and 1949, England pursued a socialist agenda that caused the economic crises to deepen even further. The English pound continued to slide in value as compared to other currencies, such as the dollar.

Eager to buttress her war-battered economy, Great Britain had, in conjunction with the United States, negotiated to build the New Aswan Dam for Egypt if she were paid in hard currency. Egypt, in return, counteroffered to pay for the dam with future exports of cotton and other commodities. Egypt then made a somewhat unrelated deal with Czechoslovakia to buy weapons under subsidized terms, part of the Communist agenda to spread influence in the Middle East. The deal angered Great Britain and the United States, who saw it as a threat to Western influence in the area. They threatened to pull out of the New Aswan Dam project if the Egyptians went through with the arms deal, so Egypt told England and the United States to get lost.

Without the revenue it had counted on to pay for the construction of the dam, Egypt now found itself in a bind. Nasser, the president of Egypt, came up with a simple solution to a simple problem. The Suez Canal ran right through his country; why not seize the canal, and the toll revenue derived from it, in order to pay for the Aswan Dam? Obviously, England and France, the owners of the canal, were more than a little put out with this. They conspired with Israel to have a short war to fix their little predicament.

Israel had been plagued by attacks from the Gaza Strip and the Sinai, both Egyptian-controlled territories. The plan was for Israel to invade Egypt. The Israelis were to take the Sinai Peninsula up to the more easily defended border of the Suez Canal. England and France were then to step in and separate the two fighting parties by seizing the canal, thus producing a buffer zone. England and France's motives were all to be completely in the name of peace, of course! In fact, England and France would get the canal back, and Israel would get a buffer zone against the Arabs. And Egypt gets . . . well, Egypt gets the short end of the stick, you might say. Thus was conceived the 1956 Middle East War.

The plan worked, at first. The Israelis agreed to the truce upon reaching the canal, but, as expected, the Egyptians did not. This gave the British and French the justification for bombing the Egyptians and landing their troops. However, the United States didn't like it. America knew what a skunk smelled like, and it didn't like the smell of a return to European colonialism. England and France could have thumbed their noses at the meddling Americans, except for one very important fact: The United States had bought large quantities of pound sterling to support England's sagging economy. As the war began, the United States threatened to sink the pound by dumping billions in sterling on the financial markets, where excessive supply would outweigh demand. Great Britain could avoid this disaster only if London complied with the demands of Washington. At first the British refused, whereupon the United States carried out its threat.

The party was over. The British were forced to agree to cease the invasion, begging the Americans to bail them out. The Americans then on behalf of the British pound supported a $500,000,000 loan from the International Monetary Fund and other measures, thus once again illustrating the Golden Rule: that is, he who has the gold makes the rules.

I use this example not to bash the British, the French, the Americans, or any other nationality. I do so only to illustrate the influence money has on nations and the people who live within their borders. A cursory look at recent history depicts, not a placid lake with tiny ripples lapping on its shores, but an ocean whose surface is tossed by billowing waves. It might be wise to own a raincoat and build strong dikes.

This brings me to a very interesting juncture in world history. Suppose some of the countries from whom we have borrowed so much decide they don't care for U.S. foreign policy. Suppose they start hinting that they might be inclined to sell more U.S. debt, instead of continuing to buy it up? Many other dire possibilities could eventually come to pass if other countries don't like our foreign policy, or if, for that matter, they simply lose confidence in our ability to keep all our financial ducks in a row. Whenever I suggest such a scenario to anyone the response I get most predictably is "Ah, we would just tell them to take a hike and refuse to pay our debts. We have the world's biggest military! What are they going to do about it, try to collect?"

One must keep in mind that more of the public debt is owned by Americans than foreigners. What happens to American debt holders if the government defaults on its creditors? I can't imagine a more surefire way of collapsing the world economy and bringing disaster down upon all of us than for the U.S. government to default on its debt. There is such a thing as credibility, even between nations. A nation throws its integrity away only at the peril of its future. I don't

175

know how such a scenario will play out, but we may all find out before too long. It will be interesting, at the very least.

I often feel incapable of affecting the nation I live in, even in a democracy. I feel like I am nothing but a tiny ant in the jungle. How can I possibly stop a herd of elephants when they stampede? It all seems so inevitable! However, that probably isn't the point. The point is, ants should build their anthills as far as possible away from where the elephants stampede.

Chapter 22
So How Would I Know?

So how would I know? My parents are middle class. I already told you my father was a lawyer. How would I know what it's like to be poor? How would I know what it's like to do without? Funny you should ask.

I'll tell it to you straight: I've never been poor. In the mid-1970s I lived on less than $2,000 per year. Subtracting books and tuition, it was closer to $1,000 per year. But I have to admit, I have never been poor. I have never been hungry except by choice; I never lived outside in the rain, and I could always get warm in the winter if I put on a jacket. Nobody lived high on the hog on $1,000 per year, not even twenty years ago. But let me repeat, I wasn't poor.

The place I lived in was the cheapest place I could find. The rent was $30 per month during the winter and fall semesters and $20 in the summer, including utilities. Later the owner had to increase it, to $40 and $30 respectively. In the summer I grew tomatoes and squash in the back garden. A friend I knew, who worked at a restaurant bakery, brought me the buns that were either too small or too big to sell. Those three ingredients, plus potatoes and carrots, provided at least half of my diet.

Two or three times I got cars. I never paid more than $65 for any of them, but I always had to get rid of them because I couldn't afford the insurance, and so forth. Dates—well, dates were pretty cheap, as you might imagine. College life was strictly business, but I wasn't poor.

It's all a matter of perspective. I have to admit that it got a bit old, and I wouldn't particularly care to go back to living on that standard again. In fact, one of the motivating influences that drives me to carefully manage my finances is the desire to make sure I *don't* have to repeat that experience. Unfortunately many Americans will, and when they are least able to deal with it physically. Over half of Americans will not be able to retire at age sixty-five. I was never poor; I was just on my way to somewhere else. Being poor is a state of mind, which I never considered. You are poor when you don't think you have enough money. I know a lot of people, people who make bundles of money, who think they are poor.

Notice I didn't use the phrase *choose* to work past age sixty-five, I said *they will have to!* What a price to pay for living like there is no tomorrow when you're young. There is a tomorrow, and you had better plan for it today. It may not be easy or fun to prepare for the future. Certainly you will be different from other people if you do prepare. However, the view is worth the climb.

I'm sure many of you are saying to yourselves, "Maybe *you* can do it, but you don't understand *me*. It's just too hard! I'm not that kind of person." Well, let me give you a clue. I wasn't that kind of person, either.

If I saw a young man today who was just like I was at age fourteen, my heart would really go out to him. I was a good young man, hardly ever in trouble, but I was a loser if there ever was one. I was extremely shy, and an extremely poor student. I am probably a little dyslexic, but for sure I was a slow learner; and due to a very unfortunate experience in the first grade, I was almost entirely unable to read. I showed my report card from the seventh grade to my daughter the other night, and she was amazed at how poor my grades were. (So was I.) But they didn't stay that way.

At age fourteen, one of my major problems was that I was sure I was dumb. I didn't think that I was simply below average; I was absolutely certain I was stupid, and I had the evidence to prove it. It is not much of an exaggeration to say that, at this point, I couldn't write anything more than my name without spelling half the words wrong. Every time I was assigned anything having to do with English, I expended at least two-thirds of my effort telling myself I couldn't do it. Obviously, most people cannot compete using only one-third their effort, so the situation ultimately became a self-fulfilling prophecy. As years went by, in spite of efforts by my parents and teachers, nothing happened to break that debilitating brain-lock.

The first real book I ever read was *Old Yeller*. It took me all day to read it. When I say all day, I mean twelve hours. I read it in the eighth grade. That summer my mother convinced me, with great persuasion, that I should take speed-reading in summer school. I protested vigorously, saying that it was ridiculous to take a class in speed-reading when I could barely read at all. Reluctantly, I accepted it as a condition for taking astronomy, my real first love at the time.

My main problem? I was spending too much time on each word, rather than thinking through the specific concept. Using projectors that show short two or three word phrases at a specified speed, I was forced to read fast enough to capture the gist of what was written. The words came so fast I didn't have time to think about how stupid I was. Since I didn't have time to be stupid, I wasn't. The summer was long, but a man-made device forced me to be smart whether I wanted to be or not. The next book I read was *The Ugly American*, which was over two hundred pages long. A few books later I read *Exodus*, which was about six hundred pages. I had broken the English barrier, just as truly as Chuck Yeager had broken the sound barrier.

A couple of summers later, I tackled earning my Boy Scout Eagle badge. I spent all summer long at it as if it were a regular job. I was a very poor swimmer, among other things, but I needed my lifesaving merit badge in order to be an Eagle. I had heard that if you take Red Cross lifesaving you automatically get your lifesaving merit badge. I took the course, but on the first day of class I was told by the instructor that there was no way I could certify because I lacked the basic skills. I asked if I could stay in the class anyway, just to practice. She said that was fine—she just didn't want me to be disappointed, thinking I could graduate.

Every day I went to those classes and came home waterlogged. You might have thought my tactic was to drink all the water in the pool, so that I could walk through the exercises in an empty pool. At the end of the summer, as expected, I did not pass the class. By the time I went to take the test from the merit badge counselor, I'd practiced so much that fulfilling the badge requirements was easy. The one requirement that scared me the most was the quarter-mile swim. I lost count as I swam back and forth across the pool. One of my friends finally had to jump in to get my attention and tell me I'd surpassed the distance several laps before.

In my senior year, I gathered up all my courage and decided to go out for a sport. I really wanted to play football, but that was absolutely out of the question. There were two things that I lacked that kept me from trying out—skill and ability. There was, however, one sport at which I thought I could make the grade, cross-country. It was the policy not to cut anyone, no matter how slow, if they continued to come to the practices and give an honest effort.

A team's score in cross-country is based on the times of

the first seven runners to cross the finish line, so extra runners are not a liability to a team, regardless of their speed or lack of it. I was the slowest runner on the Junior Varsity team at my high school. The first few days were horrible. I would go home sore in places I didn't even know existed. As the season continued, I trudged on, and my speed slowly increased. After a while I started to pass another runner, but he soon stopped coming. I guess the embarrassment of not even being able to beat Steve Johnson was too much for his pride. Once again I was the slowest.

I wasn't really running—although I thought I was. What I was really doing was jogging. Just as horses have different gaits, people also have different gaits, and jogging is definitely not running. The coach would keep yelling at me to kick out my feet as I jogged, but it always seemed like I was already doing it as hard as I could. Suddenly, during one practice, I discovered how to shift out of first gear and into second. It was unbelievable! Suddenly it was so much easier. I could run the same distance with less effort and in less time. My time improved markedly.

I was doing pretty good, I thought, as we approached the race with our rival school, Miramonte. If we beat Miramonte, the season was a success. If we lost, it was a failure. It was as simple as that!

The varsity teams ran first, and our whole team came in before their first runner. I was feeling pretty good about things when someone from the frosh-soph team walked by. He said the JV team had been packed to make sure they would win at least one race. I didn't understand, so he explained they had put some of their best runners on the JV team, even though that was supposed to be against the rules.

As we lined up on the track I could feel the usual butterflies, but this time there was a greater level of tension. I knew this was the race that would count. At that moment,

I knew the entire school was counting on me to do my best. The gun fired, and we all sprang to our positions in the pack. As usual, I fell to the back of the pack trying to keep my pace constant throughout the whole race to get the best possible time. If I ran too fast at first, I didn't have enough to keep going and would end up walking at the end of the race.

We made half a lap around the track that circled the football field, then headed off through the trees. When we reached the street, we turned left and ran up in front of the school. Past the school we came to The Hill. My coach's name was Mr. Hill, and he lived up to his name. Every practice we ran hills, hills, and more hills until we could do them better and better. When I hit the bottom of the grade I was dead last, but as I struggled up the slope I passed four or five runners who were walking. When I topped the crest, I let out all the stops and flew down the other side as fast as I could swing those feet out in front of me. I hit the bottom of the hill like a bullet and blasted across the street, where the traffic had been stopped, and through the halfway mark; one mile.

Just then I noticed out of the corner of my eye that there was someone right behind me in a green and white jersey, the school colors of Miramonte! I was tired, but I had to stay in front of that unseen runner. Several times he started to pass me, but I'd manage to pick up just enough speed to keep barely ahead of him until he'd slow down and fall in behind me again. My lungs burned and my legs were lead, but each time I'd manage to muster just enough to stay in front. Finally, as we approached the slope leading up to the track and the finish line, he made one last attempt. I tried to match him, but this time there just didn't seem to be anything left to draw on, even though the slope was gentle, only about eight feet in elevation. Yet I had run a good race; he was just a better runner than I was. He pulled ahead, and I started to slow down as the distance between us continued to widen.

I had done better than I ever had before, and I could feel it. I was used up. I rounded the corner onto the track where I could see the chute at the finish line on the opposite side of the football field. He was perhaps thirty feet ahead of me. All there was left of the race was about two hundred yards. As I started onto the track, I heard one of the varsity runners from my team yell to me, "If you let that guy beat you, we lose the race!" It was as if I had just been hit by lightning. My eyes riveted on that green and white jersey thirty feet ahead of me, and suddenly the race wasn't over any more.

I started kicking out those feet and burning up the track as if there was a lion after me. I had about two hundred yards to pass him, and I was going to do it! He must have heard me coming when I'd gotten within about fifteen feet of him, because he started picking up his pace, too. As we came down the straightaway we both kept picking up speed until we were running full out. I caught up to him just as we started into the turn around the end of the football field. The only way to pass him now was to do it in the turn. That meant I had to run faster than he was just to keep even, because I was on the outside. There was no other way, so I took the outer lane and poured it on. Our feet hammered the dirt track like pistons. Halfway through the turn we both did what long-distance runners never do, and certainly not after running two miles: we got up on our toes and sprinted through the turn.

We came roaring through that turn like a pair of run-away locomotives heading for the switch yard at eighty miles an hour. There was only enough room in that chute for one runner, and we were still side by side as we came out of the turn with only twenty yards to go. I stared at that chute, pouring everything I'd ever had into that last burst of energy, and broke through it maybe a second before the other runner.

I found out later it was the runner behind me, not the

one in front, who would have cost us the race. Nevertheless, we won, and I won. I learned that I could win, if only I had the will to do so. If there had ever been a born loser, it would have had to have been me. The truth is, several adults encouraged me and taught me how to succeed at critical moments in my life. But it wasn't until I put in the effort, believed in myself and did my best, that I quit being a loser and started being a winner. Literally, if I can do it, anybody, *anybody* can do it. Whether you have troubles with money or anything else, you *can* succeed, if you have the will to try and you learn how to win the game. The race isn't over yet, but it's time to wake up and give it all you have before it's too late.

Chapter 23
A Few Last Thoughts

In setting out to write this book I hoped to change the way you think, not just about finance, but your whole perspective on life, because ultimately finance affects almost everything, and almost everything affects finance. That is a tremendous challenge to undertake. By the time people are ten years of age they have usually already decided what is right and what is wrong; what is normal and what is not; how they are going to act; and what is important. Occasionally, a significant emotional event will occur that fundamentally changes your value system, but that happens relatively rarely. As I contemplate my limited ability to change someone's fundamental value system I am truly humbled. Perhaps some significant event has occurred in your life, and this book will act as a catalyst to bring you to a better, more complete understanding of what is important to you and what is not.

If you pay off your credit cards, or start keeping a budget, you are bound to be better off financially than you would be otherwise. My hope is also, beyond the day-to-day paying of bills, to give you a pair of binoculars with which to see a new perspective.

One of the things we have lost sight of in our modern American culture is the sacred nature of money, or wealth. By that statement I don't mean that we should worship money. I dislike being around people who do. What I mean by that statement is to respect money for what it represents, what it can buy, the price you pay to earn it, and the price you pay if you don't have it. The problem with money in recent American history is that we are awash in it; we are drowning in it. There is so much money that, instead of the many things of value that are free, we have become consumed with the trivial things money will buy.

Recent news reports are filled with stories of lawsuits, in which millions of dollars are awarded to defendants who sometimes suffer the smallest injuries, either physical or emotional. This is another manifestation of the utter disregard with which our society has come to treat money. As each legal award gets larger, what we really do is devalue money with respect to everything else. It has not always been that way, nor will it always be that way in the future.

The word *allowance,* referring to the money that parents typically give their children, comes from a very different concept of human existence. During the industrial revolution, families in Europe found themselves in crowded, dirty cities living in very poor circumstances. Their children were sent to work in factories and sweatshops. The meager earnings the children brought home helped to keep the family from starving. In some families the children were allowed to keep a small portion of what they had earned, hence the term *allowance* was coined.

I have, from time to time, heard idle conversation drift to the subject of suddenly finding oneself in possession of fabulous wealth. "Well, if *I* had the winning ticket worth ten million, I'd give one million to charity, and then I would . . ." The dreamer then goes on to indulge in the vicarious possession of luxuries he or she is not presently capable of affording, confident, of course, of being on sound moral ground, having given the first million dollars to some undefined charity.

What is missing from this fanciful frolic is the lack of realization that the person talking *is* fabulously rich! We possess untold wealth compared to people born on foreign soil. In many countries around the world abject poverty still persists, and, as a result, people are willing to take great risks to earn a few coppers. There are many people who think a hundred dollars in American currency is a fortune. Wealth is relative. You could change suddenly from a poor person to a wealthy one simply by taking a short mental trip to a Third World country. Think of all you have, not all you haven't. As it has often been said, "Happiness is not how much you have, but how much you enjoy."

On one occasion when our oldest daughter didn't get her way, she complained that we didn't care about her and said she was running away from home. She soon got over it, but the next night I arranged to have her run away from home. I went with her, of course, but she ran away from home nonetheless.

As soon as I got home from work, we left. We were both hungry, since neither of us had eaten dinner, and she mentioned that she'd missed dinner. In fact she was getting pretty hungry. I asked her what else she missed. Her sister, her mother, the dog, and her stuffed animals topped the list. I drove out in the desert to a small town with boarded-up stores and gas stations and abandoned mining shacks. Mindy is a determined little soul for a nine-year old, and pretty sure of herself, when she wants to be. But we spent quite a while wandering around the desert talking about the various things that happen to girls who run away from home, and about how these young women have lost the protection their parents would otherwise provide. As the sun set and the shadows grew darker, Mindy seemed more and more anxious to get back home, back to the place she had threatened to run away from the day before.

On the way back to the car I showed her how to find food in the dumpsters behind the old gas stations, and how to look for a place to sleep in the abandoned buildings. Mindy was not impressed. She was, however, very impressed with the hamburger I bought her when we finally got back into town. She was also very expressive of her gratitude for her mother, when Laurel greeted her at home some time after 8 P.M.

I include this experience to show (a) how an individual's view of life can be changed by seeing how dependent they are, and (b) what it is like for the many others who are so much less fortunate.

A person wasting large sums of money on trivial personal entertainment is almost as repugnant to me as someone who burns flags or plays leapfrog over the graves at Gettysburg or Normandy. Maybe I am taking it too far, but I see so much that needs to be done and so much being wasted. Anything that is received with little effort is usually little appreciated. Our Founding Fathers pledged to the American Revolution their lives, their sacred honor, and their fortunes. Yes, money—crummy, lousy money. Along with blood, it is the stuff of which nations are built.

Many factors have combined to produce the concept that money is of so little worth. Obviously, overindulgent parents, a natural product of the difficult 1930s and 1940s, fostered the flower-power generation of the 1960s. Many other factors played a part, but one that has generally been overlooked is the insurance offered both by private companies and the government. A friend of mine, who was concerned with the plight of the poor and needed some work done around the house, went to the unemployment office to find someone to work for him. Despite offering more than the minimum wage, he could not find anyone willing to work. Finally, after more than doubling the minimum wage, he found a person who was willing to work one day, but who refused to return the second day to finish the job because "it was too hard." The homeowner finally finished the job himself.

Unemployment insurance, as well as other forms of insurance, has diminished the negative effects of almost all financial difficulties. Confronted by a gun-wielding assailant, we are counseled to give our car to the thief in order to protect our life. What other rational response is there? "If you lose your life, what good is a car; and besides, you have theft insurance, don't you?" The result, of course, is that car-jacking has become more common than hitchhiking; cars are of no value. If armed, someone can take your car from you simply by demanding it.

That is not always the case. In the Los Angeles riots some shopkeepers stood on top of their stores with loaded guns, willing to kill or be killed in the act of protecting their property. They likely understood that they ran the risk of finding themselves in jail for defending their property, or even of being killed by an assailant's bullet. But they were protecting a critical part of their lives. Insurance does not cover damage resulting from war or civil unrest. Had the shopkeepers not prevailed, they would have lost the portion of their lives they'd spent trying to build their businesses.

I believe the ability to insure anything against everything will become ever more elusive, and the realization that money is limited will be increasingly more obvious as time goes by. "It's only money" may fade from the common parlance, just like "That's swell," or "Groovy!" When that happens, it will be more socially acceptable to be careful with money.

Another abnormality in history, possible only because we are presently so wealthy, is the removal from almost every action of the concept of personal responsibility. Again

I refer to the legal system as an illustration of my point. A person picks up a running lawn mower to clip the hedge, cuts off several fingers, and sues the lawn-mower manufacturer. Of course, he wins. A woman burns herself with the hot coffee she bought at a fast-food store. She sues, and wins on the grounds (no pun intended!) that the coffee was too hot. On appeal, the value of the settlement is reduced, but the total is still over $400,000! Whatever happened to taking personal responsibility for our actions?

If we are to survive as a people, we must change. The course we are on will destroy us as a nation if we don't bring a little more sanity back to our world. Look what has happened as a result of the sexual revolution. By degrading the power of procreation, from a sacred obligation between two people who pledge to remain together for life and take on all the responsibilities associated with parenting, to a mere plaything, to be indulged in heedlessly with no thought of the consequences, we have brought upon ourselves deadly diseases, which devastate millions, as well as a generation of broken families. Without a working model of what a family should be like, how can single teenage parents create a stable environment for the next generation?

If we are to survive, we must revere self-control as a virtue, not as a chain to bind us from experiencing all there is to indulge in. Spontaneity can be enjoyable, and within certain bounds makes life interesting rather than boring. But unbridled passion is not the way to lasting happiness. We must stop thinking of people who work for the future, learn, and do their homework as nerds and geeks! People who save for the future are not money-worshipers and Scrooges.

How about you? Are you willing to change? Let's see how difficult it really is. I often hear people claim they are too busy to run a budget. I am, too. That's why I devised such a simple plan to manage my money. When I pay the bills, a task which otherwise would take twenty-five minutes now takes me twenty-eight. I need to subtract each check from the appropriate category in my budget; other than that, the process is the same. When I go shopping a two-hour trip to the stores now takes two hours and four minutes, because I need to subtract the receipts when I return home. Once a month I enter the allotted amount into each category. That takes about ten minutes. It would take less time, but I usually take a moment to see how we are doing. Does that sound like a major inconvenience?

Most people treat their finances as if writing had never been invented. Can you imagine how difficult it would be to be illiterate? I don't have to imagine—for most of my youth I was. Yes, you can survive; I did it, but it isn't easy. Writing down your finances is as important to getting to your destination as reading signposts on the freeway.

Making a plow is a relatively easy thing to do in engineering terms. You don't need a lot of fancy mathematics or extensive testing to lash a few pieces of wood together and hitch an ox to it. Making an airplane is significantly more complex. You can't throw things together and just wing it, if you'll excuse the expression. The Wright brothers had to invent the wind tunnel in order to glean the data necessary for building the world's first functional plane.

To go to the moon NASA had to invent a practical computer. Not only was it necessary to make the calculations for in-flight course corrections, computers were necessary just to build the rocket. NASTRAN is the name of the finite-element analysis computer code devised to perform the calculations of stress and strain on the rocket structure, calculations that could not have been done without the aid of a computer.

If you want to plow through life, you can do so without a budget. If you want to fly, you need to do more planning.

If you want to reach a distant financial goal, you can't keep track of your finances in your head!

The more you want to have financial security and reach certain financial goals, the more you need a budget. If you don't care where you wind up financially, you don't need a budget. You'll get there—I guarantee it.

A friend of mine, one of my most constructive critics, put it this way while talking to a third person. "You don't have to do everything Steve recommends to run your finances, but I can guarantee you success if you do."

What you've seen in this book is really not new. Even though I dreamed up my budgeting scheme to solve my own problems, I really only reinvented the wheel. Almost every concept presented here is simply an expression of the same philosophy that came naturally to your grandparents or great-grandparents as a result of the hardships they endured in the Great Depression. I wasn't so smart. I came to the same conclusions others have come to when times were hard.

At a predetermined point in the classes I teach, I take a wad of twenty dollar bills out of my pocket and "accidentally" drop it in front of someone in the class. Apart from getting attention, it is always interesting to watch the reaction of the person who is now confronted with the prospect of being a couple of hundred dollars richer! I ask the person what he or she would do, on finding the money; if they knew who it belonged to but no one else did. They always respond that they would take the money back. The class quickly agrees that the only honest thing to do is to return the money.

I then ask them: If a person lies on the train tracks and waits until a train comes, is that suicide? It doesn't take long for the class to agree that it *is* suicide, even though a train is not coming at the moment the person lies on the tracks. It is not the fault of the train for hitting the person, even though the person is stationary on the tracks and the train hits them.

A rational person would stay off the tracks when a train is coming.

I then suggest to them that if they know that financial disaster, either personal or general, is a reasonable possibility, and they do nothing to prepare for it, then it is not an accident. If you take welfare that was set aside for truly needy people when you could have prepared but lived the high life instead, then you're taking someone else's money. That money was set aside for a nobler purpose. It's just as true as if you'd taken my wad of twenty dollar bills. That may seem harsh to you, but it didn't to your grandparents. Most people in their day did anything possible to stay off the dole. They would take any job they could rather than take a handout. Obviously, that isn't true anymore.

One reason for this change in attitude is that the government has now become the main source for charity in America. Having given to the Salvation Army once, most people don't have any problem with the concept that they don't expect the Salvation Army to pay them back. But with the government, it is easy to justify oneself by saying, "I pay taxes. They owe it to me!" If it is an insurance policy, the government is not collecting enough in premiums to pay for all those policies, not with more and more people committing financial suicide at an ever-increasing rate.

Suppose you lend money to someone. Suppose that person declares bankruptcy. Who pays you back? No one! The money is gone. More and more people are considering bankruptcy as a financial strategy, rather than as a last resort for those who are devastated by circumstances beyond their control. It isn't right. It isn't fair. It isn't moral.

Set your own course. Don't follow the lemmings over the cliff. Decide what your goals are and devise a plan to reach them. The difference between a power plant and an explosion is control. Take control of your money. Take control of your life. It's the winning ticket.

Epilogue

I opened this book facetiously by thanking a babysitter for giving me the desire to stay out of debt. The story is true, but there are, in all seriousness, truly a multitude of people who have made this book a reality. I would like to thank as many of them as I can for their invaluable help.

First I would like to thank my wife, Laurel, who had faith in me when few others did. I am sure that without her unending encouragement, I would have given it up long before this book ever saw the light of day.

I would also like to thank my two living daughters, Mindy and Michelle. In the words of Mindy, "Shhh. Daddy's working on his book. Let's play in the other room." They also gave me some of my best material.

My brother, Eric, was my best editor and an honest, constructive critic. I wish to thank him deeply.

Many others read my book in manuscript, and every one gave comments that helped me to complete the work. They are Jerry and Kristine Dodd, Brian Smith, Jay Butterworth, Denise Husk, and Lloyda Wilkins. I received technical advice on teenage-speak from Aubrey Wilkins and from Holly and Aaron Marshall. To all of them I wish to express my gratitude.

Many others gave me ideas I included in the book, too many to remember them all. I thank them collectively.

Finally I would like to thank my parents most of all, because they loved me.